ENCOURAGE

Jane Schnell (signature)

Jane Schnell
PO Box 326
Rabun Gap, GA 30568

Milner Press
2012

Also by Jane Schnell

Changing Gears
Bicycling America's Perimeter

Crackers & Peaches
Travels in Georgia

Both Are Better
Travels in Britain and France

ENCOURAGE

Travels
In

Siberia & Mongolia
With
World Ride Stage 9

Jane Schnell

Milner Press

Atlanta 1997

Published by Milner Press
at Books and Cases
800 Miami Circle Suite 100
Atlanta, Georgia 30324
Tel   (800) 788-9107
FAX   (404) 237-1062

ENCOURAGE: Travels in Siberia and Mongolia with World Ride Stage 9.

Printed in the United States of America.

Milner Press books may be purchased for educational, business, or sales promotional use. For information, please write Milner Press.

First Milner Press edition published 1997.

Cover, book design, and maps by Hans-Peter Guttmann

Body type is 12/14.4 Elegant Garamond

Library of Congress Catalog Number: 96-80515

ISBN 0-9626112-3-9

Our thanks for the use of references and quotes from Lonely Planet's *Mongolia—a Travel Survival Kit*; and, from Vantage Press, Inc., Dr. Christine DeWeck's *Siberia, Outer Mongolia, Central Asia: Crossroads of Civilization.*

This book is dedicated to future World T.E.A.M. Sports events

Contents

Acknowledgements

At THE GALA DINNER celebrating the last day of World Ride '95, my place card was next to Colman Rice. As we rose to leave, he and his wife thanked me for sharing stories of my journey on Stage 9—the last week in Siberia and the first week in Mongolia. Mr. Rice was so genuine in his appreciation that I began to wonder how I could represent the 225 participants who rode support stages to those whose help did not afford the opportunity to go along. We needed to thank the thousands who kept World Ride rolling and fueled by funds, labor, and cheery encouragement.

Thus, I decided to write an account of my experiences featuring stage riders and staff to accompany the splendid CBS video *The Possible Dream,* narrated by Charles Kuralt, featuring the core riders.

I came to World Ride after it was in progress. Unaware of the five or more years of preparation, I had neither attended any orientation nor met any of the participants except one, before Stage One ended in Washington, D.C. Thus, lack of knowledge and skimpy training were part of my handicap. The other was being one of the oldest bicyclists, perhaps the oldest woman.

This book, then, is my way of saying thank you for enabling me to take part in Stage 9, for encouragement to keep on keeping on, through your participation in World Ride '95. I am grateful for every pen or pedal stroke, every nickel and penny, every thought and prayer, every hand clap, and every person running to watch.

The long list of acknowledgments begins with sponsors for the ride. There were no sponsors for the book. I have overridden editorial advice against the use of brand names in the text to express my personal gratitude to corporations and the businesses they represent. However, not all sponsors are included by name.

People were like products in their contributions to this book. Coca Cola sponsorship, for example, included PowerAde powder, rarely mentioned in the text, but we drank more of it than anything else. It sustained our lives during the ride. We added it to our steaming boiled water and drank it at every temperature: hot, warm, tepid, and cool. We never mounted our bikes without filling our PowerAde-emblazoned water bottles and thermal jugs. Individual bottles of drink were carried to our meal tables, our beds for overnight sips and early morning swigs. Similarly, there were people who assisted and sustained the ideas, writes, rewrites, and production of this book, and I thank them.

Since I tend to skip over lists of names in books containing pages of them, I'll print my short list for special thanks: editor, Sara Fisher; assisting editors, Susan Goudy Gabus; Julia M. Shivers; commenting readers: Joyce A Carver, Hans-Peter Guttmann, Dr. Sally M. Hotchkiss, Janis L. Knorr, H. Peter Guttmann, Julie Milstien; consultants: Laura Herrmann, Janet Hass.

Original photographs were taken by the author, except those by Patrice Gaudin on pages 4, 44, 67, 106, 111; and by Chris Noonan, page 62. Computer work to render the photographs as Pattern Screens, produce maps, as well to lay out the book and design its cover are among the contributions of Hans-Peter Guttmann. My thanks to each of you and many others for making this book.

World T.E.A.M. Sports has no responsibility for this book, but I am indebted to Executive Director Steve Whisnant and his entire staff nevertheless. Thank you, Steve, and every person mentioned in the text. Thanks also to The Washington Post for publishing the photographs and Mary Lou Tousignant's article that set me off on this rich, exciting journey of discovery, adventure, and encouragement.

As the world's fourth largest insurance group, AXA was the title-sponsor to AXA World Ride '95. Supporting an around-the-world bicycle tour involving able-bodied and disabled athletes was how AXA encouraged self confidence and self reliance among people globally.

Encourage, the book title, is a one-word summary of the goals of World Ride '95. The author chose the title from Steve Ackerman's thought expressed one morning before we began to pedal. Steve selected *courage* as his word for the day. "An important part of courage," he reminded us, "is how we give it to others. That's *encourage*. I want everyone today," he continued, "to keep in mind, not the courage others credit us with, but our mission, by example, to *encourage* others to do great things, to rise to individual challenge."

During its first eight stages, core riders and staff had fine tuned the daily routines, but readjustments occurred frequently, especially as each new group of stage participants joined core riders and staff. We stage niners scrambled those first few days to learn the slang, learn names and faces, functions of the core group traveling all the stages, and to accomodate ourselves, to get the drill right. Get up, pack up, breakfast, load up, thought for the day, ride, break, ride, lunch, ride, break, ride, prepare to stop, room assignments, unload, prepare for dinner, dinner, prepare for tomorrow, bed, sleep, get up and do it all again, figuring out all the while where we fit into this group.

We participants observed the day-to-day courage of the core riders and the other disabled individuals who didn't get the glory but had many obstacles to face and did so daily. I had never known handicapped persons and certainly had never lived among them. As our bicycle wheels rolled and our feet or hands rotated propelling our cycles forward, each person carved an individual role to which my account gives less attention than to recording the group spirit. Perhaps others, like me, were inarticulate about their own role as we wheeled along. Some fell in love during the ride, others deepened emotions with absent persons. Fatigue often dulled interpretation of experiences as they occurred. We knew we became a mobile village, though I never heard it voiced. I probably was not alone in wondering how I was so fortunate to be there and whether or not my participation fit expectations. I felt more a misfit than a team member, more an outsider than contributor, more a spectator than a participant. Some of this feeling reflects my nature. Sometimes I felt critical more than supportive and anguished that others would notice my failure to merge. It was a most individual journey, like life, despite experiencing the same company, weather, and road.

Please realize this book was written to complement *The Possible Dream* video which concentrates on and highlights the core riders. *Encourage* intends to give more focus to the 225 bit players who were there, for the benefit of all those workers behind the scenes making World Ride '95 happen, to get it rolling, to keep it going, and those who supported World T.E.A.M. (The Exceptional Athlete Matters) Sports programs since 1995, and who continue their efforts into the future.

Prelude

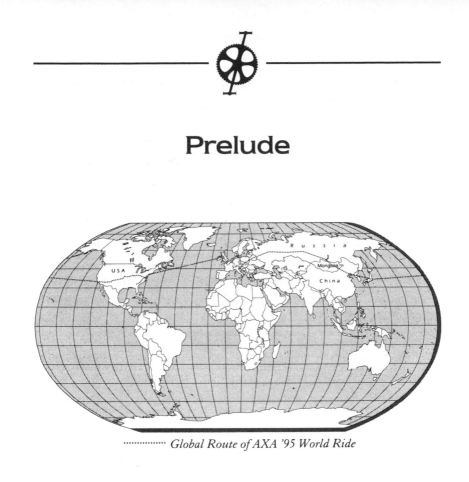

············· *Global Route of AXA '95 World Ride*

I WAS SITTING QUIETLY in the Aeroflot waiting area of Kennedy Airport, savoring a vacuum moment between two intense experiences. One was getting here; the other would begin in a matter of minutes. I let my mind scroll back through the events that had brought me to this point.

It started with a headline in the *Washington Post*: "Global Trip Puts Cyclists' Mettle to the Pedal: Disabled Riders Will Travel Through District, Virginia Today on Journey Around the World." The photograph showed three handcyclists in specially made chair-like cycles with hand-pedals. I set down my coffee cup and read the article describing a 13,000-mile bicycle tour of the world, 8 hours a day, 6 days a week, for 8 months. Seven core riders would cover 16 countries, accompanied on each of the 14 two-to-three-week stages by able-bodied and disabled participants who would raise money for the privilege.

I read the article three times with mounting excitement. "The intent of AXA World Ride '95, as the $4 million event is called, is to showcase the abilities of athletes who are physically or mentally challenged." One of the core riders, Ronne Irvine, was asked why he was doing this.

"Because maybe it will inspire some young disabled person who sees the cyclists roll through town. Besides," he added, "'can't' is a four-letter word. I don't believe in 'can't'." Ronne laughed. "The night before we left," he said, "my fortune cookie told me, 'Now is the time to try something new.'"

I knew Ronne Irvine. I'd taken photos of him and visited him in a bicycle shop where he worked as manager-mechanic. I'd watched him race and talked to his friends. He is so modest that I only learned of the races he had won from his friends or competitors.

End of Stage 1 at the Tidal Basin in Washington, D.C.

I dropped the rest of the paper on the floor and headed to the Jefferson Memorial to see Ronne and wish him well. And I wanted to meet the rest of the individuals involved.

A few people awaited the riders at the Tidal Basin. They were World T.E.A.M. Sports staff members, vehicle drivers, representatives of the U.S. Department of Transportation, stray cyclists, the media folks, and family and friends of the riders. During the wait I learned that participants need not be disabled to ride a stage, and that there were spaces open on a few of the later ones. Ellen Stone, marketing director for the ride, gave me a flyer and urged me to call for more information.

Now the cyclists arrived! Shouts and cheers exploded, refreshments and hugs followed. This was the end of Stage 1, begun 10 days earlier in Atlanta, Georgia. At last I met the core riders. David Cornelsen was telling someone, "This tour is about so much more than a handful of disabled cyclists fulfilling personal dreams. The world will open itself up to us as we connect with its communities." Then he explained to a kid how his hand cycle worked.

"Do you live on this bike?" the kid wanted to know.

"No. I live in a house, like you, but mine is in California."

I looked at Rory McCarthy making large figure eights with his hand cycle to demonstrate how he steered it—partly with his weight, partly with the wheel between his legs and pedals in front of his face. He told me he had muscular atrophy in his legs and could only walk with crutches. "But," he said, "my whole life has changed since I first discovered I could participate in sports and recreation."

A person with a microphone stepped in front of Rory, so I turned around and heard Agnes Kearon explaining that the use of her left arm was lost in a motorcycle accident fourteen years before. She has all the controls for her bike on one side and rides with the useless arm strapped to her body. She was saying "I'm not much different from other people. I have a physical obstacle, other people have less visible constraints, like time, responsibility, or attitude. We can overcome obstacles."

Agnes Kearon

A few minutes later I joined another group around one of the riders. Kathryn Rosica, from Falls Church, Virginia, was explaining to a journalist, "Participation in this event is a personal challenge and an expression of the values I grew up with and which I strive to live by. I attended school in an experimental program that brought kids of differing abilities together. As the only able-bodied core rider, I hope to continue this experience of sharing abilities and facing challenges during AXA World Ride."

In the distance, I noticed Ronne Irvine doing a video interview with the Washington Monument in the background. I walked that way, thinking of his many racing victories. He participated in the Barcelona Paralympic Games and was looking forward to Atlanta. He was saying, "It just doesn't equate in my mind that I am limited. Missing a foot and a few fingers just doesn't slow me down."

Steve Ackerman rolled by on his Freedom Rider Hand Cycle, for which he is a sales representative. He works at the Craig Hospital in Denver introducing recently injured persons to the recreation and sport of hand cycling. He told me that he believed, "Communities of the world hide their disabled population. During this World Ride I hope to show disabled people what they can do."

Watching, listening, I felt myself in awe of these people. What a challenge! At the same time, a question began to itch deep inside me. When I reached 55, I retired from 30 years of government research and celebrated the event by pedaling the perimeter of our 48 contiguous states—the mileage was comparable to what these people were going to do. For my 60th birthday I pedaled my bike across America. I was going to be 65 soon. Could I? Would I?

The earliest section I could join was Stage 9, a 600-mile, ten to twelve-day ride marking the group's last week in Siberia and first week in Mongolia—from Irkutsk to Ulan Bator. Would March to August be enough time to train? I knew I couldn't keep up with strong tour riders—but handcyclists go much slower. Maybe I could get fit enough in time.

Participating would be my opportunity to support, to enjoy, to learn about these people. My greatest joys are travel, new people, new places, and new experiences—and here they were—all in the same package. How could I resist? I'd ridden in groups with a greater mix of ages but never with such varied capabilities. Recreational tours seldom include either novices or top-quality racers, and handcyclists are rare indeed. Cycling ability isn't the issue. In week-long, cross-state rides, we begin and finish as we please, traveling always at our own pace. It would be different, quite different, to ride all day

Ronne Irvine

in a group that keeps together. I hoped I could do it.

Once I made the decision to go, things moved quickly. I phoned Allison Ariail, registrar for the World Ride. She put my name in the last slot for Stage 9 in August. Mentally, I was on my way, motivated to train for the next four months. Later I was informed that Stage 9 was full. I stopped training. A mistake was discovered and corrected. I was on the list again and resumed training, angry that I had stopped.

My focus shifted away from these reflections as the Aeroflot counter opened. Travelers began to fill the pre-boarding area. The Stage 9 riders were surely here, but which ones were they? Actually, they were easy to pick out. They all had backpacks or clothing

Ronne Irvine, Bob Roark, and Jim Benson

(T-shirt, cap, logo pin, or jacket) identifying their connection with the AXA World Ride. They all looked very fit—and young.

One of them stood taller than the rest, and the cluster around him seemed to stand straighter in his presence. I guessed he was Jim Benson, President and Chief Executive Officer of Equitable Life, founder and Chairman of the Board for World T.E.A.M Sports. Jim was listed among the sixteen participants of Stage 9.

Well, it was time to step out of the bleachers onto the playing field. I took a deep breath and walked up to a blond woman in designer denim.

"Are you a cyclist?" I asked her.

"More like a car driver, but I'll cycle some. I'm Laura, a friend of David." David, I thought. Yes, one of the hand cyclists I had seen in Washington.

Before I could ask another question, two other people rushed up to greet Laura, and soon the three were chatting and laughing. I gathered they had been together on earlier stages in Europe. The man turned to me. "I'm Terry," he said, "and this is Liza. We're your team chiefs. It's our job to get you safely to Irkutsk."

"Are you Jane?" asked Liza, smiling. Her voice was soft and warm, like the touch of a friend. She checked me on her list of participants.

The loudspeaker announced another hour's delay. Some of us started wandering here and there, while others sat and watched the bags. I met two other stage participants, Mary from New Jersey and John from Maryland.

"Are you excited?" asked Mary.

"I'm not sure whether I'm excited or crazy," I replied, grinning.

Mary Ford

"I guess we all feel that way," said John.

I had noticed that John walked with an odd bounce. Someone asked him about it.

"That's my prosthesis," he said. "Looks kinda like a wagon spring. The attachment at the ankle is called flexfoot; it's supposed to give a bit of natural spring. I lost my foot and part of my leg from gangrene after an auto accident in 1976."

"Isn't gangrene pretty rare nowadays?" I asked.

"Well, you see, my car rolled down a bank. My foot was impaled on a splintered bit of a tree. I wasn't found for two weeks."

We gasped.

He could see and hear the traffic on the road above him, but after two days of shouting, he realized that no one could hear him. He attached mirror shards from the wreckage to a tennis racket and tried to bounce reflections off

John Fahner-Vihtelic

the road signs above, but no one saw them. He kept alive by tying a string around his shirt and throwing it into a nearby stream, then wringing the water into his mouth. Using bits of wire, metal, or glass, he tried for days to cut the wood piece that held his foot. At last he succeeded. His amazing story had been written up in *Reader's Digest* (March 1977).

Some of the staff and repeat participants were talking about a Pole named Bolek, who had ridden with the group in Europe. He had no hands. Bolek steered his bike by putting his arms into cups, changing gears with his chin. He spoke no English, but had such a winning personality that they were arranging for him to ride across the United States with them when they pedaled east from California. I walked into the plane convinced I was going to learn from this group.

During the flight Liza walked around, visiting with us and swapping stories about other participants. Sitting near me were Chris, who coached swimming, and Tom, a triathlete, both volunteers with the Special Olympics, and Peter, a founder of World T.E.A.M. Sports. Liza told us we would meet the Alpha team, four men hired by World T.E.A.M. Sports for our protection throughout Russia. Their real names were long and unpronounceable, but the core riders and staff had during the past three months in Russia called them Dmitri, Papa, Nikolai, Sacha.

Our plane churned steadily east nonstop to Russia. I couldn't believe I was really going there. As a government employee for thirty years, neither was I allowed behind the Iron Curtain nor could I have flown on a Russian-built plane. The more I learned about Russia then, the less I had wanted to see it. Now sitting in this throbbing machine, I realized I still wasn't interested in Russia but was going to demonstrate my support and interest in the core riders and to share the goals of World T.E.A.M. Sports World Ride. I wanted to show that the exceptional athlete matters by trying to be one. I couldn't quite believe they had let me come. Always athletic, I'd never felt competitive, thus never considered myself an athlete. I never won anything for I never tried. As usual we talked, dozed, ate, walked around the plane, and tried to touch our toes or shake out our cramped limbs. Aeroflot carried us packed in the tourist cabin not unlike other long flights, though it felt a bit more third world than western style, more like a country neighborhood grocery than a showcase super market.

WALKING OFF THE PLANE into the Moscow morning, my World Ride pals started looking for a money exchange window and discussing currency rates. The baggage carousels began to turn and our group moved that way. I looked for a baggage cart. For the few occasions I expected to need money, I had brought fifty one-dollar bills and a few other denominations—nothing larger than a twenty. Confidence that I could get along by barter had built up during previous experiences. Even if I paid too much, hassle would have been avoided. A few seconds of observation and two dollars got a cart right away. We piled as much luggage on it as we could then rolled it outside. Two young men, redheaded Chris and dark haired Tom, heaved our baggage on the bus. We found seats and slid our backpacks from shoulders to laps.

Terry, Liza, and John were delayed. I did not realize that John's baggage had not arrived. The rest of us were quite busy hauling our mountain of luggage into and out of the hotel's shuttle—about 20 big blue and white sports bags from our Reebok sponsors. There were bicycles, too, in boxes, to replace bikes broken during an earlier stage. Novotel's modern high-rise building with glass elevators stood in stark contrast to the grubby airport terminal we had just come through. Right behind us Liza had rented two rooms for the day, one for the men and one for the women. Our plane to Irkutsk would leave that evening for another overnight flight. She suggested we store our luggage and shower or nap in the rooms, or catch the Novotel shuttle to downtown Moscow near Red Square.

While Terry and Liza coordinated John's lost bag search and attended to other details, we had a few hours to see Moscow. In a light drizzle, we sleepwalked from the shuttle drop off to Red Square and back, including a stroll through St. Basil's Cathedral.

Street repairs necessitated under-street
crossings, which was as close as we ven-
tured into the famous subway stations.

Some of us wanted to see
the GUM department store, but
no one knew how to find it. I
didn't say anything but was
sure that I remembered
from pictures that it was
opposite the reviewing
stand. I headed that way,
toward a block-long
building encased in scaf-
folding, its entrances on
the square closed. Sev-
eral others came along.
Following locals, I went
around the corner and
found an entrance with
Russian writing over the
doorway through which
passed a large amount
of foot traffic, including
women carrying sacks.

At St. Basil's Cathedral in Moscow

The last word on the sign over the door contained three letters. I
guessed, then announced "This is GUM, right here." We joined
the throng in a single file.

Inside was a several-story-high vaulted ceiling with a balcony
opening all around. Remaining on the ground floor, we gawked at
food, toy, and other stalls in front of shops, some of which were
open. We roamed around for a while, squeezing among the people.

None of us had eaten lunch. It was mid-afternoon. Our throats
were dry, our appetites mounting. Only about half of us had any
rubles, and none of us could speak Russian. We found a vendor of
bottled water which we craved. Someone tried to ask the price. Out

from under the counter came the pencil and paper. A number was written which we discussed, then decided it less than Novotel. We bought and drank. We wanted food, something to eat, anything. We found a vendor who accepted dollars for a greasy-dough pie with meat inside, one per dollar. The lady sold them all, but after two bites I was looking for a place to throw mine. We squeezed through the people back into the street, and headed for the place a few streets away where we had been let out of the shuttle bus.

Outside the Kremlin wall under a few trees ran a pack of wild dogs. They appeared to avoid people and hung together sniffing and marking the same trees and poles as they scavenged. I wanted to throw the remains of my meatball to them, but I was afraid of causing a scramble or fight. Later when I passed a trash receptacle, I shoved it in.

The ride back to the airport took the same route, Leningradskoe and Leningradskij. Walking around Red Square, climbing through St. Basil's (I liked the outside better than the inside), I regretted the lack of time to enter and tour the Kremlin. Nevertheless, it was long enough for Moscow to hook itself into my desire to come back and see more.

After rest, clean up, and peanut butter & jelly snacks, we congregated in the hotel lobby to catch a shuttle that would take us to Sheremetyevo-1, Moscow's domestic airport, two-and-a-half hours before our flight time. I met the two French cyclists who were joining us, Patrice, a young man who appeared to fit right in with our young men, Tom and Chris, though he spoke little English; and Jean-Louis, his blind tandem riding partner. Since no one else was talking with them at first, I tried my French, and we began to talk.

Jean-Louis sometimes held onto Patrice's elbow or was planted in a chair or placed his hand on the edge of a wall where he waited until Patrice returned. I marveled at his confidence. His face was quiet. Jean-Louis couldn't read our body language. I had been told that boredom was a blind person's greatest difficulty. He could neither see the person-to-person glances nor enjoy people-watching. He could not recognize people until he learned their voices. His mind had to be empty of the two-thirds of communication that is nonverbal.

Standing in the lobby, I didn't hear much of the chatter among individuals. I felt much as if I were trying to watch *Lois & Clark*, *Nature*, *Wheel of Fortune*, and *McNeil-Lehrer* all at the same time on separate TV sets while surfing the sound on low volume. Looking around me I sensed that members of this group felt a little nervous, a little lost. Money, language, and customs were strange. More than that, at home they were leaders, in positions of command; but here, in a Moscow hotel lobby, they had no one to lead, nothing to command, no jobs to organize. On the other hand, if the unfamiliar situation made us uneasy, it also tended to meld us English-speaking strangers together.

Liza came through the doors to announce the arrival of the shuttle and to urge us outside in preparation for boarding. We scurried out, dragging bags and backpacks. There were more Reebok bags than people. Our bike boxes had already been stacked out front. While some of us stood guard, others relayed bags, helped Jean-Louis, or called a companion out of the small shop in the lobby. My thought was to buy gifts on the way back when we had an overnight stay, and after I had disposed of bulky cracker boxes and weighty peanut butter and jelly jars.

We waited together outside the terminal, our luggage piled on the sidewalk. A man and girl came walking through the crowd. I noticed them because they were dressed better than others and were holding hands while talking. They walked right into our group. He introduced himself as Sergey. She was Jean, his daughter. His English was easy to understand. Jean's English was quite American.

Liza said Sergey would be interpreting for us, and

Sergey and Jean Shestakov

Jean would help. They were traveling with us to Irkutsk. Liza went to check if John's Reebok bag, which had been located in New York, had arrived at the other terminal. She would catch up with us tomorrow.

Finally we were boarded, and the plane took off. Waiting time and flight duration are poor measures of distance. I had read that Siberia is one-and-a-half times the size of our 48 United States. We landed at Irkutsk (11 time zones and two flying nights from home) early the morning of August 15. Stepping down from the plane I wasn't sure whether it was morning or afternoon. We were met by several core- and stage-staff members who helped us shove our bags and ourselves into vans vacated by the departing Stage 8 riders.

Irkutsk, Siberia

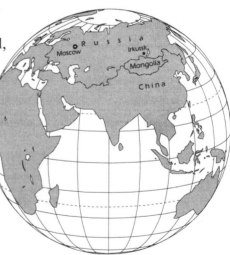

ON THE DRIVE to our hotel, I rode in a van with David and Laura and a couple of the four Russian guards —the Alpha team wearing gray camouflage fatigues. The Alphas were World Team multi-stage staff members for the five stages (three months) that the World Ride spent in Russia.

I gazed through the van window son the drive to Hotel Intourist at many ancient wooden houses, some of them vividly painted green, white, cream—fresh colors like Easter eggs.

At the hotel, Mary and I were assigned to share a room overlooking the Angara River, a park, and our vans. The day was sunny and cool, invigorating enough to keep me awake. The hotel was of

Soviet vintage similar to several I had known on a bicycle tour of Poland and Slovakia the previous summer.

We ate in a fine dining room, serving ourselves at a buffet. Finally, at lunch there was a chance to talk a bit with Ronne. He told me several people had asked him, "Can this lady really ride a bicycle?" He paused, a smirk in the corners of his eyes.

"What did you say?" I asked—perhaps with some alarm in my voice.

"Watch her," he replied.

At our table I met Bob, another handcyclist, and his wife Gruffie from Colorado, who were joining our stage. Bob and Gruffie team-teach democratic principles in Africa and Eastern Europe to leaders trying to learn to be "democratic." Gruffie explained that they teach more skills than anything, such as how to be a team player instead of a dictator. "Things most of us Americans think we already know," she winked. They had come a few days early to kayak and camp along Lake Baikal, returning to town today.

Agnes Kearon, a core rider I had spoken with at the end of Stage 1 in Washington, sat next to me. I took this chance to tell her how inspired I was by her ability to ride so far and change gears with one hand. I really wondered how she managed riding

David Cornelsen and Laura Herrmann

with one arm, since I get quite tired leaning on two of them. Agnes' eyes glinted, "You get used to it."

Bob Roarke and Gruffie Clough

Paul Curley, director of operations for World Ride—which to me meant the lead road marshal—spoke to us about road etiquette. We were to ride in parallel pace lines, staying as one group. We would stop, start, and eat, on group signals. At the borders of local areas there would be twenty-minute ceremonies when we would be offered bread and salt welcome speeches. We would have police vehicles ahead of and behind us, and would generally be led by the hand cycles during departures, arrivals, photo shoots, and going down hills.

Hand cycles are unable to climb hills as fast as single bicycles, so their pace on the road is different. We needed to give the hand cycles space, as they must track three wheels instead of two in line. We should draft, a resting technique of riding in the wind of a lead bicycle—or cluster of bicycles called a peloton—and if we do not know how, we should learn. Most important in drafting is that there should be no overlapping wheels because, if the bicycle in front swerves, it is the one behind that will fall. If you are drafting, the person in front should know it, and you should to be to one side or the other with no wheel overlap. Nothing should be done in a fast or jerky manner, and each rider should be aware of where the others are located at all times.

He went on to explain that our normal method of travel would be to ride one hour, pit stop a few minutes, continue for two hours, then have lunch. Afternoons would follow much the same routine. Of our four white vans, *Space Case*, named for the container on top, and *Bag Lady* would probably go ahead with luggage to make sure arrangements were in order. Or, if they stayed behind, they would ride through during the day as required by their duties to support the group, often sharing lunch on the road. The other two vans would follow the cyclists for safety: the medical van known as *Mash*, which would also carry riders' day bags (small personal knapsacks), and the mechanic's van known as *Tool Time*.

Siberian House

Ronne was the mechanic and would normally be the last cyclist, followed by the vans. Team leaders would carry radios, and one or more cars would have radios so that everyone could be in contact. Negotiations with locals would be handled by the team leaders, that is, staff. However, it was important to realize that as guests of the country we would often have to do as police or local officials insisted.

Paul ended by saying, "This is a ride, not a race. No one gets brownie points for overexertion. Tomorrow is our first day. The staff understand jet lag. Our vehicles are capable of carrying the bicycles and a number of riders. It is expected that we judge ourselves so as not to burn out on the first day but pace ourselves. It is no disgrace to ride an hour or so in a van. In fact, on this stage, there are not enough drivers, so that a staff member might welcome the opportunity to ride a bicycle too, if someone else wishes to drive. It takes a few days for a new group to shake down. Don't get over-tired, because on a trip like this a person can't recuperate. This ride has many purposes, and one of them is to have fun."

After lunch we made appointments to come to Ronne's van, *Tool Time*, to be fitted to our bicycles. In the late afternoon there would be a bus tour of Irkutsk. Ronne held a full-time job as mechanic during the trip. He not only cared for the bicycles but for the vans and other equipment as well. He had lost a foot and two fingers in an auto accident, and for a time had lost hope and will. Now he was performing two jobs, mechanic and core rider. Ronne had yet to ride anything but his bicycle. "I belong at the back of the pack," he said, "in case of trouble." He had the rare privilege of doing exactly what he wanted. Ronne may have been disabled, but he's lived more fully than many able-bodied people.

We helped bring the bicycles from a garage at the back of the hotel to the vans parked in front. Ronne gave me bike number 18, one of the new bikes that was my size. He had already unpacked and assembled it; now all he needed to do was put on my seat, adjust it, and give me pedals suitable for touring shoes. The pedals had the old-style mountain bike toe clips like the ones I use at home. He didn't want me to attach the aerobar, which can be dangerous in a peloton, dangerous because balance is slightly more precarious, and the brake handles are less accessible. I knew better than to doubt his judgment, even though my hands hurt a lot since my last accident when I slid on a metal grate bridge, catapulted frog-like off my bike, and landed on my knee and wrist. That flight resulted in a broken kneecap, shattered arm bone, and dislocated hand. Repair included a carpal-tunnel operation. The clip-on aerobar would have permitted them rest. To compensate I wore two gloves on that hand. Fortunately, the knee worked fine.

Sean was helping the French with their tandem bike fitting. He had lived a while in France and spoke French. Sean, a core staff cyclist, was

Sean Carithers

responsible for the radios; he also helped Ronne with the bikes and Paul with road marshaling.

Irkutsk is the main trading center and richest town in southern Siberia. It was not frozen in August, looking instead much like southern Canada and the Upper Peninsula of Michigan. East meets West here in the faces of the people on the plane, in the airport, and in the hotel. An important station on the Trans-Siberian railroad, Irkutsk is 5,191 kilometers east of Moscow. We were not far west of Lake Baikal. Further east, branch rail lines that originate in Vladivostok and Beijing converged.

Our tour guide told us that Irkutsk is the oldest city in Russia, settled originally by nomadic tribes. We got out of the bus to look at the site where Russian Cossacks in 1661 founded a fortress at the junction of the Angara and Irkut Rivers. That fortress became a hub for trade in the region. Caravans brought goods from Mongolia and China, river trade came in from the West, nomadic horsemen rode in from all directions to buy and sell. The first Trans-Siberian train arrived here in 1898, assuring the town's future. Trade consisted of furs, teas, silks, woods, minerals. Schools and churches were built and traditionally large fairs took place here until World War II.

Nothing of the fortress remains on the river bluff except a church originally built partly into the fortress wall. Today it has an onion tower and paintings on its outside walls. The fortress area is marked by a flame as a memorial to the victory over Germany during the war. Nearby are two more churches, one with steeples under restoration, and the Catholic church begun by Polish rebels sent to Siberia after their defeat by the Soviets. The latter was not used as a church until recently. It now holds Catholic services. Our guide rattled off a list of places and events that resulted in rebels being sent to Irkutsk. One of them was the Decembrists of 1825 whose ill-planned coup against the Czar failed. The leaders were hanged, but participants were sent here. Many of them were lesser nobles who stayed in Irkutsk even after they were permitted to return to Moscow or St. Petersburg. Most of the 20th century gulags that Siberia calls to mind were located further north.

We walked down a stairway to the edge of the Angara River, hung over the railing, and looked at the water flowing by at four miles per hour (about the same speed as the Mississippi at New Orleans). It had a long way to travel: 1,151 miles from Lake Baikal to the Arctic Ocean.

Paul, Chris, and Laura at the Angara River

Most of the wooden houses we saw in Irkutsk, our guide said, belong to single families and have for generations. He called our attention to symbols on the outside, usually above the windows: circles to repel evil spirits. In the old city, everyone descended from our bus and decided to walk back to the hotel along the river bank. Some went to market first. I took the shortest route and photographed a few of the houses.

When I returned to the hotel, Mary was already in our room. She is reserved, careful, and quiet, and, like Chris, works for The

Equitable, one of our major sponsors. She rides a mountain bike at home in New Jersey, as much as 80 miles in one trip—indicative of a strong rider. (It was the ride's end before I learned that Mary had lost over 100 pounds in preparation.)

By dinner time we were meshing into a group and enjoying each other, judging by the mixtures at each table. But jet lag had caught up with me and I headed for bed, missing some introductions and announcements. Russia was growing on me; as I fell asleep I could almost hear strains of Borodin dancing in my head.

Stage 9

August 16 – 26

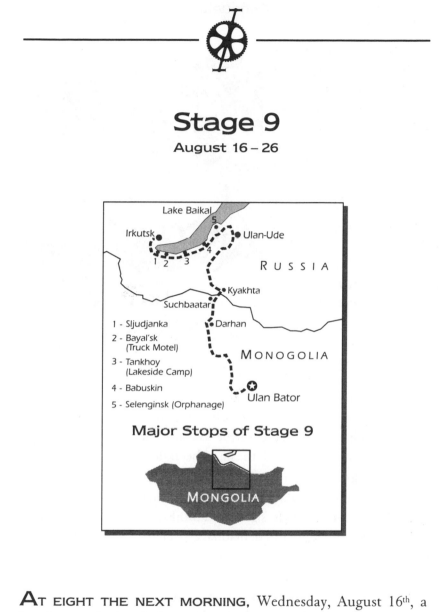

Lake Baikal

Irkutsk

Ulan-Ude

R U S S I A

Kyakhta

Suchbaatar

1 - Sljudjanka
2 - Bayal'sk
    (Truck Motel)
3 - Tankhoy
    (Lakeside Camp)
4 - Babuskin
5 - Selenginsk (Orphanage)

Darhan

M O N O G O L I A

Ulan Bator

Major Stops of Stage 9

MONGOLIA

AT EIGHT THE NEXT MORNING, Wednesday, August 16th, a band was playing below our window on the hotel terrace. It announced the beginning of Stage 9 of World Ride's 14 stages 600 miles in two weeks. Breakfast was at nine, and we were to load bags before eating. We were scheduled to pedal from Irkutsk to Sljudjanka on the southern shore of Lake Baikal, 68 miles, with departure at 10 a.m.

Mary showered first while I reorganized and tried to zipper my bag. I had filled my water bottles the night before. We dressed in our too-tight jerseys with too-tight sleeves. Core riders Agnes and Kathy recommended we cut the sleeves out as they had done. But each of them had several jerseys; with only one jersey each, we were reluctant. Riders were expected to wear the yellow and wine uniform jersey daily. If the weather turned cool, we'd be cold without

Laura, Peter, Agnes, and Kathy

sleeves. I followed Mary's attitude. "I'll just wear it," she said, scowling at her image in the mirror. We knew it couldn't be helped, for a shipment of cycling clothes had been delayed.

At breakfast I ate two soft-boiled eggs and several pieces of chewy brown bread, salad, and an orange. Bread types ranged from white to dark brown, rolls, slices, and hunks. I preferred the brown, but all of it was chewy and delicious, especially while sipping cups of hot tea.

Out at the vehicles I helped walk bikes from the garage and pump tires, although I was still a bit unsteady from jet lag, in spite of having slept for at least ten hours. Most of us concealed nervousness rather well, partly by looking for ways to be helpful and cheerful.

In the parking lot, Paul urged us to line up behind the handcyclists, to stick together, and close up any gaps. He then taught us to pronounce the Russian equivalent of *Thank you* and *Good-bye*, which we should shout to the hotel staff and other onlookers on his count of *one* and *two*; thereupon we were to mount our bicycles and begin to roll slowly into the street. A thought for the day was presented: to give courage, to encourage others.

When all was ready, Paul signaled and we shouted, led by the core cyclists. We—about 30 cyclists including a few locals—followed as they began to creep behind the police escort. Our vans drove close behind our bike wheels; then came plain security cars and more police. We were in two parallel pace lines for the first few miles. Whenever the space between us became too big for drafting, I felt more comfortable. I chatted with Patrice and Jean-Louis as we rode beside each other.

Rolling through town I could risk sidelong glances at the parks, the river, and the streets lined with old wooden houses, refreshed by new bright paint. I kept looking at the track my bicycle had to follow to keep its proper position in relation to those around me as we moved together in the flexible peloton clump.

The day was sunny and cool, cloudless—a wonderful day for cycling. In shorts and a jersey, I was cool before riding until I worked up a little body heat. The river surface seen from our seventh-story window had glittered, and it continued to look glorious from my bicycle.

As we rolled along I felt splendid and bubbly like the champagne air—clear and crisp. We wheeled past more wooden houses, past factories and heavy industry and Soviet-style apartment blocks, through tree-lined streets on the outskirts, into the forest. I glimpsed occasional wooden dachas among the trees. The forest of fat, dark, spindly spruce, fir, Siberian cedar, and elegant birch soon surrounded us. As in European forests, there seemed a dearth of undergrowth unless it grew, like bracken or ferns, close to the ground. These were the wooded steppes of southern Siberia, home of the Burjat people who live near the southern and eastern portions of Lake Baikal.

The entire day's route was flat to rolling with long passes through mountains. Blue and white painted stones marked kilometers from the last major city along the route. The white bark of the birch trees broke up the greens of pine and other evergreens while birch leaves fluttered in a gentle breeze as we pedaled a rolling, curving route, and negotiated pot holes and cracks. Gravel patches underscored the constant need to watch out for my track and those of my companions.

As clouds wafted overhead, I noticed how hard the hills were on the handcyclists, tandems, and jet-lagged new riders. Whoever rode faster had to stop often. I was one of the last up the hills. Usually I kept going instead of stopping and was soon passed by the group again.

Near the hilltop of a long switchback rise I saw Janet and Joelle riding ahead of me. Janet, a Special Olympics coach from California, piloted a tandem with Joelle, her student. As I watched they wobbled, as tandems do when they proceed slowly uphill. The slower a bicycle goes the harder it is to balance, and I noticed how much heavier Joelle appeared than Janet. In male/female bicycle tandem partners, like Terry and Liza, the male captain pedals in front while the female stoker follows because balance is easier with the stronger, heavier person in front. On Janet and Joelle's machine the relationship was reversed. As I overtook them, their tandem partnership appeared more and more unstable. Suddenly, they slowed and fell over at the feet of the faster riders waiting for us. They weren't hurt, it appeared, and since Dr. John was there, I kept going past the group. Cars were stopped by police. No one was coming behind me, and the road got quite steep for a short bit. Then I began to feel sick. I was overly tired. Curve followed curve as the road ascended through trees. As no one was coming, I got off my bike and walked, pushing it. This rested me and supplied a welcome change of pace, but I began to get dizzy and felt that my body temperature was too high. I put the bike down at the edge of the road and sat in the shade. A gentle cool breeze helped, and my breathing soon returned to normal. The surrounding forest was quiet, and I felt renewed, recharged by the stillness. Even these few days of being with people around the clock was draining energy already depleted by time and jet lag. I'm the opposite of personality types who thrive on constant company.

Horns and engines below indicated that the rest of our cycling circus was on the move. I stood now without dizziness, picked up my green Fuji Touring Series bike and continued walking, pushing it until others came in sight; then I mounted the bike and pedaled until I was last. Steve Whisnant, Executive Director of World T.E.A.M. Sports who was with us a few days, offered to push me. All morning he jumped out of a van and pushed the last one or two people to get them over unusually steep humps. As executive director of the entire ride, he probably rode more planes and ran further pushing cyclists than any one else on the trip.

Steve Whisnant

Not wanting to be pushed and unable to get up the hill, I suggested holding on to the van, which I did for a mile or so until my elbow wore out and I could no longer grip; then I got inside and tossed the bike on top of boxes. Steve got in another van, but he was soon out again running and pushing one of the hand cycles.

While driving the van, Liza told me that Stage 9 was the largest group she had yet seen on the road. I had expected just the opposite, at the ends of the earth between Siberia and Mongolia. But now that I was here it didn't seem so strange. We continued in the van a few miles to the lunch stop in a lovely green meadow surrounded by forest. Sergey and his daughter Jean, who didn't cycle, Janet and Joelle, fatigued but not hurt by their several falls, rode in other vans.

At lunch Janet had an attack of dehy-
dration, chills, fever, and dizziness. She
drank, then lay down and got warm under
a sleeping bag, but did not eat much. I
didn't want to continue pedaling but did
not intend to give up on the first day. I
walked up to the road with my bike
and awaited the others. As I stood
there I was amazed by the number
of people. There were cars and
trucks for the food and servers, as
well as three police vehicles with
blue lights on the roofs, two
vehicles of Russian photogra-
phers, and several of local TV
people. Then there were security people in all types of
vehicles, including two or
three trucks, and maybe six
or so sedans, with all kinds
of people inside.

Janet Hass

I had noticed vehicles on the road facing us as though they had
pulled over, on police instruction, for our passage. That afternoon I
watched more closely. Over and over the same cars and people
passed us, then parked on a curve so one person watched as we
came and the other as we went. We were *never* out of sight of security. It was a fluke that I had halted on a big S curve to rest and been
alone. The number of people involved in watching us was amazing.
The Alpha team were watchers of our vans and bikes. They had
become close friends with the core cyclists and staff. Besides,
national and local Russians were anxious that nothing happen to us
in their territory while TV cameras ran. This high visibility show-
cased our purpose and enhanced our safety.

During lunch I spoke with Jean, Sergey's daughter, who told
me she grew up in Russia, then moved to New York when her

mother was transferred to the United Nations. Now the family returns to Russia every summer. Her mother is a simultaneous translator at the UN, and her father a businessman. Jean said that she was in school in the United States, 10th grade, and would return after the summer here. Sergey and Jean would go with us just to the Mongolian border, then return for their family vacation near Moscow.

Long climbs and descents continued all afternoon, and the handcyclists needed help on every hill, especially the several long ones with steep inclines. I needed pushing too. Ronne rode along side and pushed me when necessary. He read my level of fatigue well.

Finally I got to the top of the pass where others were waiting. Lake Baikal was visible in the background. Jim Benson had a towel around his neck and offered it to several of us who needed to clean our sweaty glasses. We could see that long welcome downhills lay ahead. On the way, we stopped at viewpoints and looked down upon Sljudjanka, a small town at the southern end of 390 mile-long Lake Baikal. There were forested mountains on the other side, much like what we had come through. Pedaling had been like a tough day in the Appalachians. I wondered how I would manage another such day. Obviously I had bitten off more than I could swallow.

Jim Benson and group halt on the road to Lake Baikal

Lake Baikal

WE HEADED DOWN AGAIN but only went around a few curves to a larger overlook. The lake extended as far as one could see to the north horizon where water met cloud, with mountains on either side. Vehicles laden with handicrafts, which I thought must be for sale, and people holding flowers, stood awaiting us. One woman held a scarf across her arms, similar to the Tibetan welcome scarf. On her outstretched hands on top of the scarf lay a large round loaf of bread with salt in the center. Sergey translated their speeches of welcome and friendship while we stood and listened; then the bread and salt were passed, and each of us broke off a piece of bread, dipped it in the salt, and ate it.

Bread and salt—Russians with Mary

Sergey filled us in on the history of the ceremony. From time immemorial man has offered the best of his household to welcome

Trans-Siberian Railroad at Lake Baikal

travelers. Gifts consisted of essential elements of life and signaled a covenant of peace between giver and receiver. All over the world, but particularly in the East, bread and salt are essential to life. Moreover, salt is well-known for its preservative nature, as a customary ingredient of sacrificial meals, and as one of the most precious cargoes of ancient caravans.

This enactment brought to my mind the old Arab saying "There is salt between us," meaning trust and faithfulness. I imagined the pony and mule caravans carrying precious salt over the Himalayas from India, centuries ago as well as today.

Meanwhile, several other locals, a few of whom were in costume, began passing out the carved handicraft pieces from the truck. There were lacquered bowls and unpainted containers of all sorts, many of them quite fragile. They were not for sale but gifts accompanying our welcome ceremony, one for each of us on the ride.

With the meeting and welcome over, Paul led *spasiba* (thank you) and *dasvidan'ye* (good-bye) shouts. We remounted our bicycles and flew down the rest of the hill through Kultak village and across a flat area at the south end of Lake Baikal into larger Sljudjanka, 68 miles from Irkutsk, where we were to have dinner. We were supposed to stay in that village overnight. The man from the Russian Savings Bank that contributed our food decided with

Rory McCarthy with children

our staff that we should proceed to another place twenty-one miles further along the road, parallel to the Trans-Siberian rail line on the east side of the lake. We were told to stop here and eat what we wanted. Soon we would proceed further. Only the fast riders would pedal the rest of the way. The rest of us would travel in a bus. Until it arrived we participated in the festivities. Some welcome speeches occurred outside, where women brought jugs of water and towels for us to wash our hands. Swarms of children stood politely by and with wide eyes noted every detail of each bicycle and of our clothing and helmets. Their smiles were as big as their eyes. Adult interest was less obvious but equally warm.

Then we moved inside the hall and took places at the table. Salad was served, and borscht. This beet and cabbage soup is a favorite on Russian menus and no wonder; it was delicious. The fruit juice I drank was also excellent. In retrospect, what we ate that evening was among the best food I remember.

We walked out to the street to wave the core riders off and returned to await the bus. Staff members said that we were going to be housed in better accommodations with showers and perhaps hot water. I got the impression that frequent changes of plan occurred routinely during the ride.

Our banquet table was laden with dishes, cutlery, flowers, and glasses. There were open bottles of wine, red and white, beer in cans, and fruit juice in pitchers, paper boxes with which to refill our juice glasses, as well as water in plastic bottles. We drank toasts, which Sergey translated, to friendship and in thanks for our welcome. Cyclists drank little alcohol, and many drank none. Our hosts were still bringing out food and filling our glasses when the bus arrived. It seemed rude to me for us to leave in the middle of such a feast, but no such feelings were visible in the eyes of our benefactors or the core people. This was a country ruled for the past 75 years by whatever the people were told to do no matter how they felt, and these people would not have survived had they gone around asking why or criticizing what they were ordered. Not nearly so disciplined, I tried to conceal my sense of shame at walking out after the soup course to climb on our bus.

At every turn of the road someone remarked, "Aren't you glad we are on this bus?" The route was steep and winding through desolate forest. Curves gave gorgeous views of the lake as sunset approached. The colors of cloud and water changed tint from hill crest to hill crest as dusk faded to dark. Right behind the core cyclists who had pedaled the trip, we turned into what looked to me like a military camp. It was really a kind of motel for truck drivers, the main users of this road. Liza was ready for us with room keys and assignments, four to each room. Women had two toilets, but the shower changed sexes every hour. I finished dressing and doing my teeth and washing clothes while one of the men was in the shower stall, in the dark more or less, for the light bulb was on my side. Shower water continued to run hot for everyone.

A second dinner was served: baked chicken, potatoes, fruit, and tea. Sitting at a table with Ronne, I asked if he thought the place was like a military barracks. "No," he said, "we stayed at some of those; this is better." We ate, then stumbled to bed.

I shared a room with Eleanor, Liza, and Joelle. I lost my towel in the bathroom, Mary lost her shorts—we all, men and women, wore the same clothes. Our uniforms were no-size-fits-anyone clothing which we tried swapping around without finding a better fit. Mary found her shorts the next morning. The towel I misplaced belonged to the motel. They surely found it among the others.

In bed I thought back a bit. For core riders, this day of travel was slower than usual. But they had been pedaling 5 or 6 days a week since March! They all congratulated us new riders, saying it was among the longest days of the entire trip and by far the hardest day ever.

Thursday morning, core riders and staff ate breakfast in a room with Jim Benson before his return to Irkutsk after lunch. The rest of us ate in the same place where we had had supper then sat outside in the sun awaiting our leaders. It made a pleasant relaxed morning. I had gained enormous respect for Peter, who works at Goldman Sachs, with presumably little time for training. He looked pooped yesterday and continued wearing his helmet on the back of his head where it would do him no good, but he pedaled the road and struggled up the hills.

Our breakfast appealed to me, especially the local fish (like trout) served with potato puree, a fresh orange, and hot tea. There was, of course, wonderful thick, chewy bread. The milk product we never identified. Speculations ran to sour cream, yogurt, clabber, or *koumiss*. Those of us who spread it on the bread liked it. Patrice and Jean-Louis ate it with a spoon.

I really admired these people, and already it seemed as though I had lived with them for a long time. Of course, some of them got on my nerves, as surely I did on theirs. Elly was so upbeat no matter what happened that I often wished she would just keep quiet, but

she made me laugh too, which
was helpful. She was no longer
Eleanor, but Elly, a good com-
rade to us. Liza was positive
and caring to everyone in a
more mature and quieter way
that buoyed each of us.

In late morning we stood
over our bikes awaiting the
signal for our departure ceremony. Steve Ackerman gave
our thought for the day in
which he spoke about the
courage others attributed to
us during this world tour.
However, he felt it more important for us to focus on our
purpose to *encourage* others to
challenge themselves and dis-

Elly Hogg

cover how much they could do rather than think on what they were
unable to accomplish. This message impacted us more coming
from Steve, the most physically challenged around-the-world rider.

On the count of *one, two, three,* said not too loudly by one of the
road marshals, we shouted at the top of our lungs in Russian,
"Thank you, good-bye," then in English began muttering "creeping"
to notify each other of our location and quiet movements as we proceeded too slowly to keep good balance. It became a jargon among
ourselves. Often we used it when impeded by the public while smiling and waving. After creeping sped to a modest pace on a road clear
of cars, we accelerated to a touring pace. After yesterday's practice,
cued by the core riders, we had the rhythm of departures—symbolic
and fun—though I often didn't want to leave.

Al and Rick had a red van that Al named *Black Cat*. It was the
TV and camera platform that took them to hilltops and all kinds of
places for their long shots of our group. Sometimes they drove

alongside with *Black Cat's* doors open, filming. We were asked not to look at them or react to their presence, just keep doing whatever we were doing unless one of them gave us directions. The vans, bought in Ireland, were intended for sale in China. In Japan they will rent vehicles for the short time they are there. The same Chrysler caravan vehicles used in the States will be driven to California to meet the group in Los Angeles for the United States crossing.

This morning we were all to stay back a few hundred yards while, from the back of *Black Cat*, Al filmed an on-the-road rolling interview with Jim about his childhood friend who motivated him to become founder and chairman of the World Team Sports. He and Ronne, equipped with personal mikes, pedaled just behind *Black Cat*, driven by Rick, while Jim told Ronne his story. We followed some distance in the background.

It was a beautiful day and a splendid undulating road with straight stretches over a mile or two long. There were forested mountains on the right and Lake Baikal on the left beyond the Trans-Siberian tracks. We saw an occasional small fishing boat on the lake, while a few clouds, fog, or mist collected here and there in layers over the water in the distance.

Lake Baikal is 49 miles wide at its widest point. We were at the narrow southern end where it was not more than 20 miles wide. Because of its depth, 5,369 feet, more than four times that of Lake Superior, Lake Baikal contains a greater volume of fresh water than any other lake on our planet. The midday temperature varied between warm and cool, perhaps in the seventies to eighties, with a fresh clean texture to the air something like that I had experienced pedaling along the Great Lake shorelines in Michigan.

While we waited for the interview to end, I rolled near the front chatting with Sean, a core staff member. Then we continued a bit faster, took a brief rest stop, called turtling. Why "turtling"? Because there aren't that many restrooms along Russian roads. For the past three months the women had waded out into the wheat fields and squatted down. All that could be seen was their cycling helmets, looking like so many turtles among the wheat stalks.

We rolled to the lunch stop in a small meadow off a side road. We were about 300 yards from the next district boundary, where Paul, our chief road marshal, said we would change police and the people designated by the Savings Bank of Russia to provide our food and housing.

A full banquet tarp had been laid on the ground in the sun. There were dishes of fish, tomato, cucumber, noodles, and meatballs served on small plates, glasses of juice, and cartons of juice for refills. We sat or stood, ate, drank toasts, and listened to speeches translated by Sergey, wandered off into the bushes as necessary, then tried to find shade under the few branches of trees that hung over the road. In my group photo there were thirty people, but Al and Rick were not pictured in the crowd. Al was busy taking the pictures with each of our 30 cameras, and Rick was busy handing him the cameras.

Then we gave our *thank you, good-bye*, shouts to all, and especially to Jim Benson who was being driven back to Irkutsk by Steve Whisnant.

While our leaders Jim and Steve waved, we crept three hundred yards to another bread-and-salt welcome ceremony at the internal Russian Federation boundary. After that short stop and speeches, we continued with new escorts.

A new cry developed, *gapping*, which meant close it up; slow down, or speed up, but stay together. In these countries it was better to ride together the way the local police preferred, which we could not have done without such experienced road marshals. Already high, my opinion of the benefits of racing skills got a daily boost from these marvelous roadrunners Paul, Sean, Ronne, Ken, and Elly.

Ahead were usually Agnes, the French tandem, Dr. John, Chris, Tom, John, Kathy, Paul, and others. Staff rotated into vans or onto bikes, but Terry and Peter were more often on the road.

The slow group included all the handcyclists and the rest of us stage participants. We maintained a brisk pace through the sun-

The road ahead

splashed afternoon for 30 miles with very few short stops. We passed an occasional village: small, neat, well-kept wooden houses with corrugated roofs, wood fences, gardens, and a few goats or dogs.

In the country again by the side of the road sat a woman, further along another, then a man, each behind a pot of wild berries or a container of smoked lake fish ready to eat. The berry pickers had fresh wild blueberries and raspberries for sale by the bucket. Occasionally a small group of people would walk out of the forest carrying their berry buckets or fish. Waving, on we rode.

I was becoming quite tired; Ronne encouraged me to draft a lot. He often got parallel pace lines going, and we kept moving. When I had trouble keeping up, he offered to pull me up to the group by letting me draft him. I did so for a couple of kilometers. We had almost caught up when his radio crackled. *"Black Cat* wants to know where we are," Ronne said. The last marker I remembered was 225. He relayed that. Then we passed 228, and he told *Black Cat.* "Good," they said, "you're quite close. At marker 231, there is a gravel road on the left; go along it under the railroad tracks and turn left, then go until you see us."

At our turn, we hit large rough gravel. I bounced down behind Steve's handcycle and continued left, pedaling over hard packed dirt with lots of depressions (potential mud puddles), then over more gravel. We picked individual tracks along the dirt road, past houses and barking dogs, for at least a kilometer to the end of the road at a clearing on the right. I wove among the security vehicles and got off my bike. We were on a bluff overlooking Lake Baikal.

I stood ankle deep in grass among our vans and stared at the bluff edge where a fire burned. Buckets hung over the fire on a log cross piece set on Y-stakes. Beyond stretched the lake, clear blue, lighter than the sky. Puffy popcorn clouds floated above; a few small boats floated on the water below. Far beyond on the other side, dark evergreen-covered hills rose from the water's edge. On either side were young birch groves. I put down my bike, walked to the bluff, and looked through the crystal water into an array of rocks on the bottom. A few of our group were sitting on the beach removing their shoes. Someone nearby remarked, "It's great for swimming too, quite warm, much warmer than on the other side where we went on our rest day." I turned around. Liza was walking toward me. "Can you believe this paradise?" I asked. Her eyes twinkled more than usual.

Liza said the handcyclists would camp there near the vehicles. The rest of us were to carry the tent bags through a few trees up to a larger open field and erect the tents. A few people had round two-person tents with fly covers. We were four to each of the large

Camp on a bluff of Lake Baikal

square tents probably intended for eating or sitting rooms. Neither square tent had a fly. Elly told us how to pitch them and insisted that no tension ropes were necessary, so we left them dangling. I looked at the clouds. Surely it would rain during the night. After several trips back to the vehicles to carry up to the tents everything we needed for the night, I wandered back to the bluff and slithered down to the water's edge.

Liza was rowing a boat with a couple of people in it and one or two others swimming alongside. Not able to resist the cool lake water, I eventually slid over enough rocks to submerge myself before returning to shore. My wet uniform felt comfortable after being hot all day. I sloshed in my shower shoes through the grass to my tent to change.

When I got to the tent, I decided to go ahead and wash since I was already wet, and took soap and a towel down the steep bank near the tent. This area was slightly shielded from most of the folks. Ronne and John were sitting on stones. They had taken off their prostheses and were washing their legs. They said the water was warmer than they expected. I went around a big rock and slid into the water, submerged as much as possible to wash inside my clothes. I longed to swim, but I felt it wasn't smart, for I was so exhausted I could hardly get over the slippery stones into deep enough water. Also I was hungry, so I scrambled back up the bank to the tent to get ready for supper.

I returned to the center of trampled grass and people amongst tents and vans parked at odd angles over the uneven ground.

The sky and water were constantly changing as the sun sank into distant dark clouds blowing our way. Rain would come, no doubt of that. We were still near the end of the lake, and the black undersides of the clouds coming over land and hills were full of water. They would meet a change of temperature when they reached the lake. I hoped there would not be enough wind to knock the tents down on our heads.

Ronne repairing a flat

We wandered about on the bluff above the lake edge. The Russians kept their fire going, while further back we tramped down the long grass waiting for dinner. Locals were making fish soup in two buckets of water hung over the wood fire.

I approached the food preparation area, wondering when and what we would be eating. Near *Space Case* van, Ronne was peeling dried fish and offered me a piece. It turned out to be excellent. It resembled the fish I had seen for sale and longed to eat during the ride. I ate several pieces as he peeled and handed bits around. We continued eating fish as the others crowded around pots of noodles and other food that our Russian Savings Bank hosts had prepared for us.

Ronne kept peeling fish for people to eat. I noticed the noodles pot was almost empty so I said to Ronne, "I'll get us a plate of noodles."

"Thanks, I'll get my own," he snapped. I stood still and ate another piece of fish while chatting with Liza about wet shoes. She accepted a piece of fish, put it into her mouth, then moved off. I tried again.

"That noodle stuff is almost gone. Could I get you some while I'm getting mine?" He glanced quickly at the near-empty pot and replied, "Yes, thank you." I had to scrape, find forks, and put a stuffed pepper on each plate before setting his down near his elbow where he could see it. I found some apple juice containers and handed him one, then looked around for a place to sit and eat.

Nearby, Patrice, Elly, Janet, and Mary washed the used plates and utensils in a succession of three pans of water laced with chlorine. There was no soap. I went to my bag, among the others on the grass, and found the small plastic container of liquid dish-washing soap that I brought for clothes. I added it to the first pan of cold water. The next two pans of Clorox water were progressively cleaner. I also found a plastic container to sit on and proceeded between bites of dinner to pass the plates from one water pan to the other, then into the hands of those trying to dry them with towels too wet to absorb more.

Elly, Mary, Patrice, and Janet were now talking about the location of the privy. I didn't know there was one and had been going in the woods on the way to the tent. "It's a hole covered by a plastic milk crate with no bottom and a toilet seat on top. There is even a plastic bag full of paper!"

"The view of the sunset over the lake from there through the trees is special, for the lake is straight ahead. Below a small bluff is a rushing stream that provides music and sound privacy."

Laura suggested, "You must go see it even if you don't have to use it." I had need of it and marched off according to directions. "Continue down the road until you see the shovel, then look left." On the return I felt much better. They were still talking about the privy and someone asked, "How do you know if it is in use?"

"When you reach the shovel you ask, or someone there will see or hear you and say something."

I drifted here and there for a time and finally went to the tent again after dark. Liza had said that we need not worry about our bags as they would be covered by tarpaulins or shoved under the vehicles in case of rain. I went to sleep in the tent where Elly and Agnes lay in the center and Janet on the opposite side.

About three or four in the morning I was awakened by water dripping on my face and all over my sleeping bag. Lightning and thunder approached from afar; that wouldn't have wakened me, but I couldn't get away from the dripping. My rain jacket was in my bag a hundred yards away. Twice I got up and stretched the tent, dumping water puddles. By then I was also lying in a puddle and extremely out of sorts. It seemed I was just back in my bag when the light rain grew heavy and woke Elly and Janet, who sat up and began talking. I stayed put, grumbling that I was so wet it didn't matter any more.

"Oh goody! This is an adventure," yelped Elly as she crawled back in her bag. I wanted to kill her. Finally, I settled down and perhaps slept a little. When I got too restless, I got up and went down to camp. One bag was sitting alone on the grass in the rain. It was mine. Well, at least I didn't have to hunt for it. The top layer of things under the center zipper was wet. I was annoyed with myself for having relied on hearsay. I was still tired, and more irritable than usual. No one was up, no food in sight. I took the large water bottle from my bike back to the tent, ate an energy bar, and drank the water while scribbling notes and waiting for our world to awaken.

Rain dripped in my mouth and on my head for about three hours no matter how I moved around. I tried to curl up in a way that avoided the drips, sleeping fitfully between 3 and 6 a.m. when lightning and thunder recurred. There was little wind. Elly got up, went out and shook the tent, then quietly returned. I wrote some notes for about an hour, then Liza coughed in the other tent. I decided to get up and move out.

This Friday morning, fatigue was not confined to my legs, as I learned when I couldn't find my jogging bra. I went around both tents searching the poles and corners and nearby tree limbs where clothing hung—turned out I had it on.

Teacup in hand, I then went down to the central area. The Russians had a fire going on the bluff, and a bucket of tea was brewing. They offered me some. I drank two large cups full and felt better standing with them. The sky overcast the lake with gray.

Someone was stirring near the food van. I found and ate a bowl of muesli and milk, with extra banana chips and raisins supplied by Agnes, who didn't like them and picked them out of her muesli. We wandered to the bluff and found Gruffie seated on a stone near the Russians preparing cup after cup of really good coffee. People were coming to life.

Back at our tent I found the women folding tents, tugging the poles apart, stowing gear in bags, and carrying loads to the vans. It took several trips to remove all the sacks, bags, and the sleeping mats from our two tents. That done, I watched my bag loaded on a van, put my backpack into *Tool Time*, and rolled my bike into center field with others who were ready to go. Paul and Sergey made and translated speeches to the local people who had assisted us overnight and provided our dinner. We shouted "thank you, good-bye," then pushed our bikes out of the tall grass to the dirt road before we began creeping on them back the way we had come. Village dogs barked behind wooden plank fences. For a time I was behind Steve Ackerman, marveling at how he manipulated his hand cycle alone through depressions in the dirt road, over bumps and grass, avoiding dung and gravel, rolling smoothly all the while.

Paul Curley, our chief road runner, stood on the road directing traffic. "Come along," he said as I gained the road, and we rode together for a time. I knew he was a semi-retired racer. (I didn't know his reputation until I got home and read his vita—it nearly popped my eyes out.)

Ahead lay a stretch of rollies, smooth pedaling and fun cycling. We moved in several short pace lines not far apart, at a steady rate. I felt so good I just didn't care about the possibility of burnout before the end of the day. I rode with Paul a bit, then with Sean a bit, but mostly behind some strong rider's wheel. We negotiated some construction and gravel that was not difficult. Light rain stopped, clouds broke up, and I drafted a tandem up a long but gentle hill. More jackets went into pockets. Before lunch Janet and Joelle fell again. Joelle at almost twice Janet's weight was simply too heavy a stoker for Janet to captain on their tandem. Joelle sprained her wrist, and the doctor told her she could not pedal any more that day. They rested riding in a van.

We had started before ten in the morning and stopped for lunch between one and two. Turning off the main road, we sprinted at will along a few flat miles to eat in Babuskin, the village where we had been scheduled to camp. Babuskin was a resort village on a bay of the lake. There lunch was served at a long table in a wooden building among birch trees a hundred yards from the sandy beach lakeside. It tasted so good that I ate too much.

As I walked past my bike, I noticed a boy looking at it. He turned, looked at me, then slightly ducked his head and moved away. That evening my watch was no longer on the handlebars. I should have known. It was not valuable, but I had worn it since the cyclists gave it to me at the end of the tour in April when I took them through the Carolinas and Georgia. It was especially useful on this trip because it had a button that lit the dial at night. The rest of the trip I went watchless.

Too soon it was time to go. I wished I had spent an hour swimming in the lake. A few did before lunch, but I chose to relax on the grass with the others, surrounded and ogled by children. We had thirty-eight kilometers to go, about twenty miles. It continued to be a wonderful ride. I got a couple of pushes from Sean as he came up behind me, then on the last big steep long hill I felt dizzy and climbed into a van.

Terry captained Liza on the tandem. I went into *Mash* that Sergey was driving. Jean and Joelle sat in front; I sat in the rear with my feet on two water coolers. Sean pedaled up to our moving vehicle, opened the sliding door, asked Sergey to "drive very steady," and gracefully placed a foot on the van floor to hold himself there while the bike rolled. He used one hand to refill his water bottle. Then he held it toward me while I poured PowerAde powder into the bottle. Sean was still sitting on his bike as we drove about ten miles an hour. "Fabulous trick," said Sergey when Sean had closed the door and pedaled ahead. Later Ronne came for water, opened the door, and asked me to fill the bottle for him. At supper that evening, he told me

Liza and Terry

that on another day Sergey had heard "slow down" when he said "don't slow down" and almost threw him off the bike while he refilled his water bottle. These racers are good!

We continued into a lovely and ever flatter river delta of farm land—grain fields—and pasture, then turned off the main road to arrive at the edge of a village just as hundreds of cows were walking home. Our hotel for the night was an orphanage. The women in our group were given a suite with a toilet and wash basin, four beds in one room, and three in another on the second floor. Liza showed us where to go, suggesting that we carry our baggage up right away and come back in fifteen minutes ready to be driven to the river for a bath. The handcyclists got their crutches or wheel chairs, and the rest of us helped with their bags or carried them in their chairs up the stairs.

Coming down again, I saw for the first time David's ingenious solo descent. The stairs were made of stone, the railing was metal and quite sturdy. David turned his chair around backwards and held the railing with both hands, allowing the chair to roll down, bump by bump, stair by stair, his hands and arms on the banister controlling the descent.

Handcyclists had rooms with beds, but all the rest of the men slept on the floor in one large room using their mats and sleeping bags. Sergey and Jean shared the office. Jean, who had apparently spent most of her life in diplomatic circles in Moscow and New York, told me that she didn't like camping. But this trip provided an opportunity to see a part of Russia she and her father had never visited. When she referred to doing her job as translator, I assumed they were paid, as were some of the staff.

On the bus we drove through town to the river, passing more cows coming in for the night. The only vegetation was low willows at the water's edge. To our displeasure, the police leaned against their cars and watched us disrobe as we entered the water. We kept our backs to them until we were submerged. Then we bathed under water, swimming around to rinse off. The problem came in reaching our dry clothes and towels. Pretty soon we were laughing so hard we just didn't care anymore. We were clean! We even waved to the police as we climbed into our bus.

Before going to my room I filled my water bottles with boiling hot water from the van (put in the insulated jugs this morning, it was still so hot I could hardly hold the full bottle), dropped in my iodine pills, and carried them to my room to cool. In the room I strung up my clothes line and hung much of the contents of my bag to dry from its overnight rain soaking. At the river we had also washed our cycling uniforms, so we hung them on the windows to drip. Our room was a mess of bags, clothes, shoes, and just plain stuff. Mary, Janet, and I were sharing. The other women, Agnes, Kathy, Elly, and Joelle were next door. Staff members slept on sofas in the room where we dined.

Dinner was soon ready for us at a long banquet table. There was plenty, and it was much the same as before: bread, potatoes, soup, salad of various types, and sometimes fruit. [Later in Dr. de Weck's book, *Siberia, Outer Mongolia, Central Asia: Crossroads of Civilization,* I found the following description that fit our Siberian meals: "Russian dinner always starts with cold smoked fish; sausage; ham; cold cuts; olives; tomatoes; various herbs (parsley and chives); bread; butter; radishes; all according to season. It is a time for welcome toasts, speeches, and a general warming-up. Usually a very rich soup (a meal in itself) follows. Then fish or meat, with potatoes and vegetables, is served. Sweet cakes with coffee or tea finish the meal."] Fortunately we seldom had it all at once.

Our usual drinks were fruit juices, sodas, beer, and sometimes wine. The lager was good, and so were some of the juices and sodas. My preference was soup and tea, with bread and jelly.

As we ate our dinner, singers and a couple of accordionists performed, which I enjoyed. The kids from the orphanage kept trying to run in to see what we were doing, and Rory and Terry, who had a way with children, led them on and gave them candies, even though adults came to pull them away. Chris and Peter folk-danced with the singers. We participants were tired and wanted to go to bed, so our applause ended with a *thank you, good-bye*, before we moved off to our rooms. Our lights were out by 10 p.m.

We had come about sixty-eight miles on the first day of riding and around a hundred the second day, of which I had probably done seventy. This day I had done perhaps sixty miles. In short, I was surviving.

During dinner the night before, Paul had announced that we were expected to arrive at the square in Ulan-Ude on time, as the grand finale of a three-day handicapped sports event there. Baggage was to be brought down and packed in

Terry, Eliza and children

the vehicles by 7:30, before Sunday breakfast. We would start by 9 a.m. to cover 130 kilometers (73 miles) on flat road with one long hill about midway. We had to arrive before 4 p.m. at the square where the largest head of Lenin in the world rests on a pedestal.

The first creeping took us through the village on the road we traveled last evening to bathe. Rolling beyond town went well. After warm up and reentering the main road, our pace picked up from seventeen to twenty or twenty-three mph. That gave me no problems as long as I drafted. We passed lovely farm land and pedaled through small villages along the river valley leading from Lake Baikal upstream to Ulan-Ude. Grain was being harvested with tractors and other large machines. In a vision from an earlier time, narrow strips of grain near the road were cut by workers using scythes. The contrast of this scene frustrated the photographer in us since we were constrained by time and the requirements for togetherness. We were compensated by the joy and ease of pedaling together on a good road without hills while we chattered like a flock of migrating birds.

Chris dancing

I drafted Ronne or the French tandem most of the day, or Kathy or Agnes, who were talking and not so steady, then rode beside Ken or Paul while chatting. I felt fine until about an hour before our lunch stop when I began hoping it would come soon. Both my water bottles were empty. Sean filled one and returned it to me. On and on we pedaled through lovely country. I thought they would surely select a spot for lunch near the river where there was space, shade, and a view of the water. We passed several such places; then, while riding through a village with especially picturesque houses, strange things began happening.

Cars behind us suddenly accelerated along unpaved side roads, careening over bumps, and winding among trees on both sides of the road trying to pass us. Brakes screamed. Dust flew and small stones were flying on all sides for we monopolized both lanes of the road. Ken shouted "STOP!" We did, pulling our bikes off the pavement into high grass. Our vehicles moved to one side, allowing the other traffic to resume normally on the road, much to the relief of the drivers, I supposed. They had had more than enough of following our group at a twelve to fifteen mph pace.

Liza came running up out of the last van. "Is this where you want to eat?" she said.

"Where's the food van?" said someone. "Where on earth has it been?"

"It's there," said Liza pointing. "We've been rolling behind you waiting for you to stop."

"My gosh," he groaned. "We've been waiting for you to tell us where to stop!"

"Well, is this where you want to eat?"

It wasn't. But by then we didn't care about anything except food. So, in a dusty grass area, with bits of farm equipment lying about, we ate lunch at the edge of the village. Six of us sat elbow to elbow on a log amid the debris. Others ambled about. Handcyclists remained in the sun and dust at the road edge dependent upon food being brought to them. While we ate, the advance police returned and worked with the following police to keep the traffic moving past us.

Within twenty minutes I ate kasha and chicken prepared hours before, then drank a couple of quarts of juice, not because it was good but because I was so hot and dry. I ate a tomato without peeling it because I couldn't find my Swiss army knife. I ate too much too fast, then ran to my bike. The group was creeping.

A few kilometers later began our long climb of about two kilometers. Except for a short bit near the top, it was not too steep. Everyone was waiting there for me and for Vladimir. He had gotten off the morning train from Karsnoyarsk, equipped with a leg and knee prosthesis that squeaked. He rode his own few-speed rattling

Patrice, Jean-Louis, Mary, Paul, Jane, and Ronne

bike in tennis shoes and wool shorts, wearing a shirt that seemed too hot. Vladimir pedaled mostly with one leg and had gears too high for the hill we crept up together. Our boys pushed him as well as the hand cycles. Some evenings Sean, Paul, and Ronne were more exhausted than I was, I think, from all the pushing they did.

As I rode with Ken again, he told me that Ronne was his best friend on the ride. They were room and tent mates, and he tried to needle and tease Ronne out of his solitary "I can do it myself" stance whenever he started digging in his heels. I didn't want to ride at the back so that Ronne would have to push me, so I tried to stay in front by drafting Ken. Gradually I believe I earned the respect of the road bosses for my few cycling skills, for commitment, and for quick learning. But there was nothing much I could do about slow recovery time from expended energy, a factor of age as well as training, time zones, and jet lag.

Ulan-Ude

WE CROSSED THE RIVER into Ulan-Ude. Once more I was fraying the last shreds of energy. Both Ken and Sean noted it and gave me little pushes on the rises. "Relax into my hand and rest a moment," one of them said, his open palm on my back. I did and soon was over the hump, able to propel myself again. They were great. I guess being able to judge the energy left in other riders must be part of winning races. These guys certainly read me loud and clear.

At the top of that hill we were greeted by a dozen or so disabled people, some in wheel chairs. The core riders stopped to greet these people, but by the time I came up to them, the whole group of World Team cyclists, locals on foot or crutches and in wheelchairs were moving slowly down the road mindful of our schedule. We mixed among our greeters, straggled along the road edge and side-walk, turned the corner, entered the square, and headed toward our advance people at the other side of it. We rolled, barely balanced on our bikes, into the square with five minutes to spare. We halted by the statue of Lenin for photos, then kept moving as Liza and Terry directed us into "the building with the horses on top," a theater or opera house where our bikes were stored in the lobby.

Janet was wobbling about on her feet. I sipped my near-boiling grape PowerAde and wished I'd filled another bottle, for this wouldn't last long. I found Dr. John, who took Janet aside to sit down. She said she was thirsty. I handed her my water bottle with perhaps half a glass of liquid left in it, then followed the others. We were ushered into front rows of seats as the curtain rose. After being outdoors day and night, the theater seemed hot, close, smelly, and suffocating. I sat gladly, but would have preferred to be lying flat on a cool marble bench or on the grass outside or even on a bed. Instead, for over an hour, I listened to music.

Soon I could hardly concentrate on the show for want of water. Then I began to feel sick. Finally it ended as John, Ronne, Agnes, and Sergey made short speeches from the edge of the stage. Agnes was last. The mike was too high for her so she extended her neck, slightly exaggerating her stance, and said in Russian "thank you," rose on tip toes and smiled saying, "good-bye." It brought the house down—they loved it, and we relished our exit.

Unscrambling our bikes took a few moments because each of us took any bike out the door into the air where bikes and riders sorted themselves. A half-mile pedal took us to the hotel garage. We walked back to the entrance and hauled our baggage up to our rooms. I lay on the bed. The hotel was not so old, and more western than old-line communist in design. A quarter hour later, looking out the window, I saw a few of our people headed for our parked vehicles in a fenced area. I grabbed my water bottles and went quickly. I got there just in time to fill one large and one small bottle with near-boiling water. Exhausted, I returned to our room.

Mary my roommate had showered and was dressing. I showered and lay down for almost an hour until supper. Still I felt sick. During dinner at the table with Steve, Paul, and Ronne I couldn't tolerate food, but was desperate for more water.

Back in our room I went to bed and soon slept. Throughout the night I awoke over and over again, the first two times to vomit and thereafter because of diarrhea. Finally I slept until Mary awoke. Then I felt all right, but empty.

I wasn't sure whether I was really sick, had eaten something that disagreed with me, or my body simply was unable to exercise and digest at the rates demanded. I put Epsom's in my water bottles for the day, just a little, for its cleansing effect. Dr. John gave me two pills he said would control diarrhea. I decided not to take them because I seemed to be all right, just weak and sensitive. I thought rest a better cure than pills and asked to drive a vehicle this morning.

This was our last full day in Russia. Steve Whisnant would be leaving tomorrow together with our four Alpha guards and all the other Russians, including Sergey and Jean. They would turn back at the Mongolian border. I could feel group emotion rising. Breakfast was replete with stories about teammating and reinforcement that what we were doing was important. The core group, both riders and staff, had been living and working with the Alpha guards in Russia for three and a half months. Now they were leaving Russia and these friends behind. Thinking about it, I realized that I too was about to leave Russia and the guards—and I had only known them for six days. Tonight we would camp near K'achta after about a seventy-three-mile ride south from Ulan-Ude.

Sunday breakfast lasted long enough for me to get down some kasha, a pancake, and tea with sugar. I still felt stable. I rode in *Mash* all day, the hospital ship driven by Liza, behind the riders. Janet rode with us, sleeping intermittently. She wasn't feeling well. Several others were sick too.

I took two bottles of water with me in the van and sipped them all day while we kept station at ten to fifteen miles per hour. As each was emptied, I filled it to cool while using the other. The first halfday I rode as a passenger. The second half, Liza stoked the tandem (pedaled the back position) and I drove *Mash*. Driving was better than just sitting. I certainly didn't feel like cycling. The route was beautiful, an alpine atmosphere, very green, with small lakes. After lunch we had our last bread and salt in Russia, followed by Russian gifts for each of us. Mine was a wooden box containing pine nuts.

By afternoon I felt much better and enjoyed the ride from this different perspective. In *Mash* I had a radio and could talk to the road marshal cyclists equipped with radios, or just listen as they talked among themselves. They talked about road speed, who was having difficulty, what was coming ahead, calls for the doctor or mechanic, driver changes, lunch stops, announced stops or starts, and so on. My respect for on-the-road management of the ride, and for individuals doing their team jobs, was enormous. I had traveled with so many different types of bicycle tour groups in the past that I knew skilled road marshals were avoiding confusions and frustrations hour by hour.

Cows watch us leave Ulan-Ude

Finally, on the radio came word that the next camp was near. The instructions directed us to cross the bridge over the river, climb the hill, take the first dirt road on the left and follow it to a right turn after a house, then continue until the tents appeared at the river's edge.

Black Cat and some of the core riders in the advance group had carried their small tents up to the top of hills and pitched them there. The rest of our tents were already pitched in the pasture grass along the river. We piled out of the vans and dragged our bags into a tent. We women spent another night in the day tents. This time I chose one of the center spaces in case of rain, for leaking was worse at the edges, even from dew. Then I looked around at our gorgeous camp site by the river. The tents were pitched in a row along its bank in trampled-down long grass. Except for the bridge we had traversed and the single farmhouse, there was nothing in sight except the river, with low fields on both sides that rose gradually to rippling grass covering the surrounding hills. I entered the tent to lie down flat for about a half hour. Refreshed, I emerged again.

A group was about to drive up to the bridge and body-float a mile down the river to camp. Ordinarily I would have been one of the first in line for that venture. I could see the water was brisk and decided that what I did not need was another physical energy challenge. So I took soap, towel, and other clothes and went to the river for a swim-bath that proved exceptionally refreshing despite the difficulty in keeping my footing in the speedy current.

Supper was served, and I went over to the table along with the first group. There was skewered grilled meat and vegetable salad, and I had a glass of ginger ale. As there were not enough seats for everyone, I wandered back to my tent, lay down, and quickly fell asleep.

It was dark when I awoke. A light cool breeze was blowing. Without a watch I had no idea of whether it was midnight or just before dawn. In my tent Joelle, Mary, and Kathy slept. The breeze and barking dogs from the nearby farm led me to think it was pre-dawn. I was zipped in my sleeping bag wearing a wool sweater and a windproof suit with lined pants and jacket, socks, and a wool hat. I was cold.

Then it was light. People began to stir. Ken walked by carrying his tent down from the hill top. I sat up. Mary was awake and said it

Riverside camp

Ken Snelling cooking pancakes

was about 7:00 a.m. We were to leave by eight for a long cycling day that required our reaching the border by two in the afternoon. From there we would have an additional twelve miles to the town of Suchbaatar, Mongolia, where we would overnight in a hotel. (The staff did a great job of ensuring we were able to wash and alternate indoor and outdoor sleeping. The main attraction at being indoors was hot water!)

Liza brought instant coffee to the tent. I sipped it as I stuffed my bag and rolled my mattress, then went to get my clothes off the line Al had rigged between two vans. They were almost dry. When I returned to the tent I put on my uniform, packed the Reebok bag, and hauled it to the van, continuing to the river on the way to break-fast. I carried along my soap, towel, and tooth-cleaning gear: cup and mouthwash in a plastic bottle.

Ken was cooking pancakes that he sprinkled to order with chopped dates, raisins, apricots, fresh apples, or nuts. He also had his own batter recipe that began with standard prepared batter. To it he added a little ginger and cinnamon. Two of these pancakes with sliced bananas and syrup earned rave reviews. This breakfast could keep you pedaling all morning. A cup of Gruffie's coffee helped too.

I hauled my bike down from the van top and put the front wheel on, then began walking up the sandy road. The front wheel scraped. It was out of alignment. I returned to the van, changed the wheel, then headed back up the road to the farm buildings and continued to the hard top road we had left yesterday. We pushed through sand patches, through which all the hand cycles needed help.

Once on the road, we waited until everyone had arrived, except the tent-striking crew. Then we began pedaling, slowly a mile or two, then drifting behind the police escort. The police vehicle stayed a quarter or half a mile ahead of us to avoid the danger of our running into their vehicles, and to tell traffic coming toward us (which was pretty sparse now) to halt on the side of the road until we passed.

The two vans behind the riders, *Mash* and *Tool Time*, blocked both traffic lanes, so that no one could pass the bicycles from the rear except when staff notified everyone by radio that traffic was coming through. The habit of riding all over the road was so ingrained that it took a while for the cyclists to move right to let vehicles pass. This style of riding was essential for the hand cycles because, with three wheels, their riders often had to steer all over the road to miss the debris and pot holes that threatened to overturn their cycles, or even break them.

The Monday morning road was quite straight and the curves gentle; hills were gradual and infrequent. We moved fast because the time for our border crossing into Mongolia was fixed. After about twenty miles my legs were well warmed up and I felt marvelous. I had been wanting to photograph the group from the front; up till then, nearly all my shots showed the riders from behind. As we came over a slight rise, I saw what I needed—a long, very gradual

Cyclists on the road

descent with a good backdrop. This would allow me to use the descent to catch up and not cause a gap or make anyone wait for me. I burst ahead as fast as I could (and almost caught the police) stopped, jumped off my bike, and snapped three shots as the group flew by, yelling and waving. Then I jumped onto my bike again—and couldn't get it going. A strange noise sounded like the brakes dragging. I got off again and was inspecting the front brakes when Sean drove up beside me in *Mash* and said, "It's your saddle bag, it came loose and was dragging on your tire." I took it off and handed it to Sean for storage in the van.

On my bike again, I began to hammer the pedals. Ronne had slowed down to wait for me, but even he was far ahead. I still had a mile or so of gradual visible downhill so I laid it on the pedals. I didn't want to hold them up. Standing, I spun as hard as I could. I was really feeling exuberant. The road was pretty smooth too. I passed Ronne, who was moving just fast enough to maintain his balance, and kept going as hard as I could, knowing that with this sort of effort I probably would burn out and not be able to ride all day. It felt so good just to *go* that I kept at it despite running out of

breath. Gasping, but still pedaling, I sat on the saddle. Gradually
I slowed the spin rate; I couldn't
do any more. But I caught the
back of the group with enough
momentum to weave among
them and get over the next rise
with them.

Later, when I drifted back
again, Ronne came up beside me.
He said, "Nice going. Sean told
me he clocked you at thirty miles
per hour. I asked him because I
was waiting for you and was
really startled when you flew by
like I was standing still. You really
surprised Sean; he didn't know
you could do that."

*Elly, Rory, and Eliza by the church at
the Siberian border town, Kyakhta*

"I had a lot of gravity help," I
smiled with pleasure, "and I may
have burned out for the rest of the day!" In fact I kept going and continued strong until another batch of rolling hills right after lunch. I
ate well but carefully: three cups of hot tea with sugar, a plate of tomatoes, bread with only one slice of cheese, an orange, and some
rice. After lunch I felt tired but not exhausted. After our break the
first hill proved to be rather long and had a few steep places.

By the top of the next long hill I was barely making it, hardly
able to draft. I lost the French tandem there, then couldn't stay with
the Terry-Liza tandem's rear wheel. A descent rested me, but on
the following ascent near the top, we took advantage of the covering
of trees and little paths to make pit stops. Sitting on a stone under a
tree in the shade, I realized that I had blown my energy for the day.
Ken was sitting nearby and realized it too. He suggested I ride in
Sean's van, for we were eight miles from the border and had to
hurry. He put my bike up.

The road to the Russia-Mongolia border carved through hills, and there was much to take in: a helicopter airfield, military camps full of tanks, trucks, and other equipment, finally the border town itself, Kyakhta.

From the top of the hill we saw the church at the border as we descended into the town. We told Liza by radio that we were coming, and she said that they could see us. Sean took to his bike, and I took the wheel. I drove right up to the barrier and stopped. I got out, locked the van, and joined the crowd milling about between the border control barrier and the church. Liza was handing out our passports with separate visas stuck in them for Russia and for Mongolia; Sergey was translating for Paul, then for the Russian Savings Bank representative as they spoke. Liza urged us to walk on and push our bikes past the barrier pike. The driver in whose name each van was recorded had to drive his vehicle through. I gave my keys to Ken and took his bike, then the four drivers shuffled the keys around and drove the vans past the lifted barrier into the holding area. One by one we waved to everyone, shook hands with Vladimir and the bank person, then entered the holding area and walked to the side of the building where we left sight of the Russian public.

Officials came out of the building and several of them inspected and stamped our visas. There were emotional good-bye hugs and exchanging of scarves and caps, even though boots and clothing were exchanged the night before. It was very emotional for the Russians and the core people who had traveled together for more than three months. Finally Sergey, Jean, and Steve, after a short speech, followed the Alpha guards to Russia with one last *thank you, good-bye* ringing in their ears. We walked

Alpha Papa and Sean

toward another barrier where our
passports were inspected again
before we entered the zone between
borders.

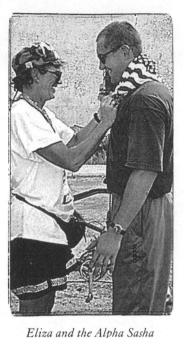

As we walked, each van was
driven over a pit and under a platform for inspection from above and
below. Ken said the inspectors took
one look in the windows and shook
their heads. There was no trouble,
and the time involved was short. We
proceeded to the center of the border
zone; the vans drove next to us.

Into Mongolia

Eliza and the Alpha Sasha

FROM MONGOLIA ahead a band
struck up. We stopped to take a group photo under the "Welcome
to Mongolia" sign, a further delay involving about thirty cameras.
Finally we moved again, and I happened to be among the first few
to pass the passport inspection men who stamped our visas and
passports. I was handed a bunch of flowers so wilted that I guessed
the people had stood there for more than the hour we were late.

Nevertheless, our greetings were as warm as the day. The dep-
uty Minister of Health came personally from Ulan Bator to meet us.
As Arabs offer dates and aromatic infusions, as the French offer a
glass of wine, as the herdsmen of India offer a cup of water-buffalo
milk, these people met us with bowls of their most precious com-
modity, mare's milk—a symbol of their esteem, linking us with the
legions of far and fast riding nomadic hordes which swept down
from these very plains and conquered the known world. They
placed blue scarves around our necks as the Tibetans welcome with
white ones and the Hawaiians with floral leis. These jovial, strong,
handsome people have a long history of physical prowess. Known

as formidable archers and wrestlers, their greatest renown has always been as horsemen.

Mongolian men held our bicycles like horses in a line while we accepted the welcome by sipping the milk, smiling, and waving our bundles of wild flowers. We listened to the band, to speeches with translations, and marveled at the glittering eyes and strong faces surrounding us, while twenty horses bobbed their heads and shook their manes. Some of us were put on the horses for photos. Meanwhile dust swirled with good will as children galloped their ponies around the outskirts of our group. Al could hardly take pictures for all the local TV and other people standing in front of any person talking.

At last we were given back our bikes. I pushed Ken's, having promised him that I would drive his van so he could enjoy entering a new country on his cycle. We walked for a hundred yards or so, then one by one mounted our bicycles. Pony-mounted people and pedestrians trailed along on both sides of us, together with jeeps, local bicycles, security cars, and our vans. After about three hundred yards the group thinned enough so that Ken jumped out of *Tool Time*, handing me the keys and taking his bicycle.

Mongolian horseman

The Mongolian police looked very spiffy dressed in black, with trousers tucked inside their boots like World War II parachutists. They waved black-and-white swagger sticks out of car windows to show their authority or to direct traffic. We proceeded through the town, horses kicking up dust on either side of the road, trailing

Entering Mongolia

fewer pedestrians and children as the bicycles picked up speed. Horses, dignitaries, and cyclists progressed about three miles to a statue commemorating the great battle for the independence of Mongolia that occurred in that area. More speeches and more mare's milk were flung about. Finally we got underway again and continued, with dignitaries in vehicles but fewer horses every mile, for the next ten miles into and through Suchbaatar to our hotel.

Children ran, and horsemen and women galloped toward the road to wave and cheer at our passing. Right away we sensed we were in a different place, a place of individualism and space, lots of space. This wasn't Montana, but it certainly was big sky country. People's cheekbones, dress, and language were different. The scenery was different: dark forest greens changed to yellow grasses, and mountains slipped to barren hills bordering a plateau dotted by livestock along the Selenge River. Rugged green grass and small streams covered the plateau where *gers stood*, and sheep and cows grazed. (*Ger* is the Mongolian word for a yurt.)

Gers are easy to recognize; they look like large white circular tents. Supported by collapsible wooden frames, they are covered by felt under the white canvas. No tree or bush obstructed my view, and the clean air made the gers look closer along the grassland valley than they were. Although they appear flimsy, gers hold up amazingly well in Mongolia's fierce winds.

We arrived at the hotel. Elly and I were in one room of a two-bedroom suite. Liza and Joelle shared the other room. Liza was busy making arrangements for a jeep to drive us to hot showers. Out came soap, towels, and clean clothes in anticipation. Two jeeps were loaded, and away we careened. Around a few corners, along one-way streets, around a series of apartment blocks to descend not more than a couple of hundred yards from where we started. The building appeared to be a sports club. We were ushered inside by two women who escorted each of us to a private shower compartment. There we showered in privacy, shampooed our hair, and emerged, along with a cloud of steam, to dress. Outdoors, we waited a short space under the watchful eyes of half a dozen spectators and children until the jeeps returned with more of our group and we rode back to the hotel.

I lay down until time for dinner and read parts of Ken's Lonely Planet Publications'—a travel survival kit—guide book, *Mongolia*. I learned that most Mongolians still live in gers, even in the suburbs of the capital city, Ulan Bator. Wood and brick are scarce and expensive, whereas animal products and canvas are cheap and readily available. Mongolians traditionally have been nomadic, and their homes can be moved easily. Depending on the size, a ger can be assembled in one to three hours. Of course, the average resident of Ulan Bator is no longer a nomad, but like middle-class Westerners, Mongolians prefer to own a home in the suburbs.

Gers are quite comfortable. Some have wood floors. In urban areas, they may have electricity, but in rural regions candles provide light. Usually a stove sits in the center for heat and cooking. In forested areas, firewood can be burned in the stove, but on the prairie the main fuel is cow dung. Toilets are always outside. If showers are available at all, they will be built in a public bath house serving a group of round white canvas-covered houses that from

Gers

across the prairie look like tops one could spin by holding the stove pipes.

Not many travelers spend much more than a day in this area, which is about the time it takes to get across the Russian border and down to the next region by train.

Our hotel was in Suchbaatar, the regional capital city, Mongolia's chief border town. Here traders spend the night on their way to and from Russia. The cross-border traffic is not what it used to be, but with the collapse of state enterprises, entrepreneurs buy cheap goods like clothing in China and sell them in Russia. Suchbaatar has more petrol than elsewhere in Mongolia, thanks to smuggling from Russia. I learned a lot from Ken's guide book.

Elly put her head in and called us for dinner. We walked to another building where a long T-shaped banquet table was laid. We liked the food, and I tried to stay awake and look pleasant during the speeches. The Mongolian musical entertainment, especially the songs with a Chinese opera twang, did help. Finally I headed for sleep.

Packs of barking dogs were running and fighting outside in the early Tuesday dawn on all sides of our hotel.

Elly spoke. "Did I keep you awake all night?"

"No, why?

"I was up and down the whole night with diarrhea."

"I'm sorry. How do you feel now?"

"Not good, but better. But I'll stay here a bit longer."

At breakfast I avoided the tomatoes and the yogurt-like dish, but relished a crepe stuffed with rice and meat, bread, jelly, and two cups of tea with sugar. Elly and a few others arrived as we began eating. Before leaving the dining area, Gruffie and Liza held a short meeting; then they announced that while the core staff and riders met, we participants could go to the museum with the translator or do what we pleased before returning here for lunch. We had a 21-mile ride today and we would leave after lunch.

We Stage 9 participants gathered in front of the hotel, where we were disappointed to learn from Jomo, our translator, that we couldn't visit the museum because the electricity for the city had been cut off. So we sat on the front steps in the morning sun: Laura, Patrice, Jean-Louis, Mary, and I, with the mayor, one of our hosts and his granddaughter, our translator, and others. We looked along the road we would travel to the capital, Ulan Bator, the same road we had pedaled from Russia. It is Mongolia's main road, two lanes, hard-surfaced, and carrying the heaviest traffic in the country—but to me it seemed almost empty.

Hotel in Suchbataar

Our translator Jomo was not busy, so I asked him, "How much would it cost me if I came here alone to stay one night at this hotel?"

"About twenty dollars," was his reply after he completed the currency calculations in a rough fashion in his head, with bystander assistance.

To our right were parked all our vehicles: *Tool Time*, *Mash*, *Black Cat*, and the two we saw seldom except when parked, *Bag Lady* and *Space Case*. Our bicycles were mounted on top and locked in place. We kept the vehicles locked. *Bag Lady*, of course, carried the luggage except our backpacks for day use, which stayed in *Tool Time*, and *Space Case* carried a lockable container on top in addition to the bicycle racks. It also carried the extra gift items such as T-shirts, pins and brochures, the cooking gear, tents, and sleeping mats for camping. These two vehicles were used by Terry, Ken, and Liza for advance contacts or stay-behind food shopping and cleanup.

Some people wanted to go to the post office, but I preferred the market. Jomo told me where to find it. Jean-Louis and Mary chose to stay where they were, sitting in the sun on the front steps

Mayor and his granddaughter

of the hotel, so Patrice and I headed off to market together. It was neither far nor crowded. People stared at me, perhaps because I was wearing shorts, perhaps because we were curious foreigners, obvious westerners. Products for sale were for household utility, clothing, or food—candies and vegetables. The meat was laid out on tables in a large room with open, unscreened windows. Outside were several tables of freshly baked bread. The women bread vendors would not permit photos. When I lifted the camera to my eye someone shook their hand at me and turned or ducked. We stood and watched without giving offense, then circled around a couple of times and departed.

On the way back Patrice wanted to find the post office. We walked in the direction I had seen the others take, across a large square, the town center, but I didn't see the post office. Patrice recognized a girl he had talked with at the hotel. In answer to our question about the post office, she led us to it.

Patrice spoke French and a few words of English. MG (the Mongolian Girl) spoke Mongolian and a little more English than Patrice. I spoke English and a little French. Armed with all our science, we approached the lady behind the counter. She spoke Mongolian.

Patrice told me he wanted 30 stamps to send post cards to France. I told MG. She told the lady. The lady smiled, said something, and opened one of her stamp drawers.

"Wait a minute," said Patrice, "I don't have any Mongolian money. Will she take dollars?"

I asked MG, MG asked the stamp lady. The stamp lady smiled, said something to MG. MG told me, "yes." I told Patrice "*oui*." So

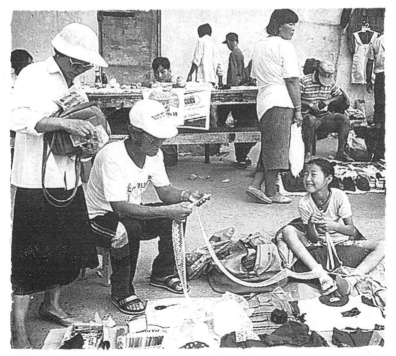

At the market

Patrice naturally asked how much 30 stamps for post cards to France would cost. I asked MG. MG asked the stamp lady. The stamp lady frowned slightly, consulted a chart, and from somewhere under the counter pulled out—an abacus. Click, click, click—and she told MG the price. MG told me. I told Patrice. "But that's in Mongolian money," said Patrice. "How much is it in dollars?"

I scratched my head, then asked MG. MG shrugged her shoulders, and asked the lady. The lady threw up her arms, then grabbed her abacus. Click, click, click —and the information passed to MG to Jane to Patrice. Patrice brought out his dollars, the lady brought out her stamps, and the trans-action was concluded. Oof!

Jane with the Mongolian girl

The only trouble was that the lady, while giving Patrice his change (in Mongolian money—she was a wonder), showed us some interesting post cards of the region. I decided I would like to buy some of them—and we were off again.

This time it was much quicker; only three people and two languages were involved. In a matter of mere minutes, I had the post cards, including some for Patrice, according to our side deal, and some Mongolian change; and the stamp lady had some of my dollars. We started for the door, with thank yous and smiles of mutual understanding. Patrice had been leafing through his Mongolian change. Now he stopped us.

"I'd like to have some of these Mongolian banknotes as a souvenir," he said. "Do you think she has any clean ones?"

I asked MG. We returned to the counter. Suppressing a giggle, MG asked the somewhat surprised lady. The lady began to grin. Then she nodded. MG nodded to me, I nodded to Patrice. He produced three worn-out bills and, ignoring our newborn protocol, handed them directly to the lady, who gave him three crisp clean ones. MG and the lady, still grinning, exchanged a long glance in Mongolian.

All this had taken some time. I looked over my shoulder, wondering what would happen if other customers, possibly in a hurry, should come in. Surely, in a busy town like this—? No one came. We had the lady all to ourselves.

Then I realized I had post cards without stamps. But we had a routine now. Accompanied by more giggles and repeated calculations to reduce the change and ensure the same number of stamps as post cards, I was finally satisfied.

As a matter of fact, by now there were two post office ladies. I never knew whether our lady called her colleague over to join in the happening, or whether the colleague simply didn't want to miss any of the fun. But there they were, grinning as only Mongolians know how to grin, and eager to see the next act of our comedy. MG was beginning to shake with restrained laughter.

Patrice was putting away his 30 stamps and his clean Mongolian bills. I was putting away my post cards and stamps. We were ready to leave.

Not quite. I didn't know what to do with my left over Mongolian change.

"Patrice," I whispered, "How much change do you have left?" He opened his hand and looked. I looked. We counted. With great effort—and without abacus—we calculated. Between, us we had enough. MG and the two ladies waited expectantly; what would these strange visitors do next?

Pouring our combined cash into MG's hand, I asked, "Could we have two American dollars back?"

Choking, MG translated and smoothed the bills on the counter. Still grinning, our lady handed two one-dollar bills to MG who handed them to me. I handed one to Patrice. The colleague, still grinning, was counting out the Mongolian bills.

Thank yous and good-byes, *bayartai, bayarllaa*. As we closed the post office door behind us, I thought I heard laughter. I joined in. So did MG and Patrice. Still chuckling, we headed for the hotel. I asked MG if she lived here. She did not. By now Patrice and I had worked out a series of nods, shrugs, and eyebrow language interspersed with a few spoken words to indicate whether we understood each other or not. The result was that the English to French translations became rather staccato and word oriented rather than whole sentences or whole thoughts. MG lived in Ulan Bator where she was going to the university and came here by train for a few days to visit her parents, the hotel owners. I thanked her for her help. She said it was nothing. A dollar remained in my hand after all our transactions. I gave it to her. She looked at it and shook her head. I said, "You earned it. We could never have bought our stamps without you!" She tucked it away. Mary and Jean-Louis were not in sight at the hotel. Jomo our translator motioned us to hurry. We thanked MG while Jomo urged, "You are late, come quickly to lunch." He set off at a jog walk; we followed.

Our meal consisted of three courses, a salad and two meat and vegetable dishes. I drank several sodas and one cup of tea before I slipped out. On the way I put my head into the kitchen, camera in hand, but all the women waved their hands at me. I focused on the pots and they moved out of range, then I rubbed my stomach and smiled, saying what I hoped was sufficiently close to the Mongolian word for "Thank you." We learned to do our "Thank you, goodbye," in Mongolian the day before but had to be prompted each time, quietly, before shouting. Every one of us seemed to pronounce the words differently, but our audience got the idea and shouted response to our efforts.

Our departure did not really begin at the hotel, for all the people watching us ran the few blocks as we rode, creeping behind the police vehicles to the highway, then into the big square that we had walked across on the way to the post office. The square was now full of people, and a band struck up as soon as we appeared. The mayor, holding his granddaughter by the hand, spoke of welcome, thanks for coming, and good luck on our journey. Ken conveyed thanks for making our visit so pleasant and allowing these meetings of friendship to occur. Finally, "thank you" in full voice, a pause, "goodbye," and softly among ourselves, "creeping, follow the cars and keep left, creeping, creeping, mind the people," as we pushed our bikes until the people moved, while we nodded and smiled, and finally mounted and crept. Once we were all on the highway, we rolled slowly in our usual fashion to allow everyone's legs to warm up until the buildings were behind us. Children ran alongside us as far as they could, and we knew by now it would be several miles before the individuals on horses that looked like ponies came to a halt and watched us cycle out of sight.

Our ride to the next place was supposed to be twenty-one miles. It turned out to be more like thirty-two, but still a short day. There

The Mongolian cyclist accompanies Steve and David

were a few long hills though. Along the way, we were astonished that a Mongolian man who joined us at the border was continuing. He cycled wearing a prosthesis on each arm and on one leg. He rode a one-speed bicycle quite well. Usually he rode far ahead alone, near or drafting the police vehicle. Not knowing his name yet, Kathy and Agnes referred to him as the Bionic Man. It stuck. There were several local vehicles and occasional kids on ponies alongside the road. We were the traffic. We pedaled through a pine forest as we climbed a hill, and the rest of the time rolled through valleys alongside mountains or through foothills covered by grass. There was nearly always a ger or two or three in sight. We followed valley after valley through an area that raises a multitude of animals.

About one-third the distance from our destination, I grew nearly crazy from riding the brakes down the hills to keep with the group. I had about decided that I was completely fed up with this dog-and-pony show and only wanted to go home. Just then we were divided into fast and slow groups and told we could proceed as we wished. A couple of miles down from a pass, rolling free with the breeze in my hair, I felt marvelous and lost all my attitude and hostility except for the pain in my hands from bumps and pulling on the brakes. Suddenly it became a truly *great* day! On the flats again, I was content with my place in the slow group with Gruffie, Bob, Janet and Joelle, Ronne, and the core handcyclists.

Eventually we turned off the main road, then a mile or two later proceeded through a village. Just before another small hill we

Our road

Halt in pass

stopped for everyone to fill water bottles from the van and for David to rest his aching back. He did this by flinging himself out of his hand cycle and lying flat on the ground while Sean massaged his back. Villagers collected nearby to watch us—some of them on horses. Suddenly Liza appeared galloping over the hill on one of those pony-sized horses followed by her escort, a proper gentleman wearing his Mongolian clothing and hat. He also carried a black-and-white police baton. She told us that we would be camping just over the hill. The villagers had erected a ger just for us; they had even dug and built a two-hole privy on the side of the hill. "You're almost there," were the words I most wanted to hear. She wheeled her horse, shouting, "I'll tell them you're coming, you're gonna love this place," and galloped away.

After getting around the hill, we could see our vehicles and the ger on the slope a quarter mile above the village. Liza and her escort were galloping into camp. Some pedaled up the dirt road, and others, like me, pretended we were on real horses and pedaled straight across the grass to the camp. We stacked our bikes against each other or on all sides of a couple of large stones near the ger, where we were summoned for cheese, sodas, the mare's milk ceremony, and speeches. Of course it took us a while to get herded inside and seated on benches and the floor. We were excited and delighted to see a ger up close. Including our hosts there were forty-five people inside and a number of small tables and benches. It was also hot, so we all worked up a sweat sitting still, even though they left the door open and enlarged the hole in the roof. Getting us outside again was easy.

On the way out Ken was next to me. He said he found this ger fascinating. "I'm an architect, you know. This really interests me. I wonder how they got the opening larger while we were inside."

"Come on, I'll show you," I said as we stepped through the door into strong wind. We walked around the ger, and I showed him the ropes used to open and close the roof. Ken was surprised. He said, "How did you know that?"

"Well, I used to import Tibetan rugs from Nepal and I was active at a few Textile Museum functions. One of our members owned a yurt, from Iran or Afghanistan, I think. He set it up in the museum garden for special events. I was there once while it was being put together and I thought it was interesting. These are only different in detail, not in concept."

Supper was ready for us now, and we were driven down the hill to the village bar, where we sat inside and were served wonderful soup, then stew. Ronne came in, all smiles and quite excited. "My hands were greasy from working on the bikes," he said, "so I took my water bottle outside to wash a little. There was a man standing there. He watched a minute and then went away. He came right back with a pan of water and soap and even a towel. How about that!"

In the bar we were unable to open any windows and were seated quite near the kitchen. It was so noisy that Sean, sitting across the narrow table, and I, sitting next to Ronne, could hardly hear the exciting story Ronne was telling about shooting himself in the leg with a .22 pistol when he was young. His father was a gun collector, and Ronne knew how to handle guns. But while he was checking the greasy pistol it slipped and went off. The bullet went straight through his thigh. The wound, only a small hole, did not hurt because he felt nothing at first, but he knew he had to get help before the shock wore off. He did. And he was back on his bicycle in a matter of weeks. I realized that Ronne had displayed a cool head and enormous self reliance and discipline from a young age.

Several of us inspected the windows again. They were nailed shut. I assumed this was a winter necessity for there must be long periods of wind and bad weather. We sweated through the meal. I began to feel sick so I went out without dessert. I wish I had recorded what we ate. I do remember that it was delicious, especially the bread.

Waiting outside, it was chilly in the wind, so I stayed on the side of the building that shielded me from its direct force, thinking about what Sean and Ron had told me about the Alpha boys. Employed by a private protective agency, they carried a lot of ammunition and from time to time did some practice shooting. Holding up his wrist Ronne said, "I came very near giving Nikolai this watch even though it was given me by my father. It belonged to grandfather." I realized how close the bonds between the Russians and the Americans had grown during the journey across that vast country. Sean and Ronne shared equal depths of feeling about the Alpha security four. They were hoping that it might be possible for the Alphas to come to Washington for the final ride day, but since they were not cyclists, that seemed unlikely. (Two did come.)

Before long the others came out. We climbed into jeeps and cars again and were driven past the ger area to the top of the hill. We were met by the museum keeper who dressed like a holy man. He took us into the museum. There were stuffed deer and other animals, rocks, and photographs of the area. We liked best the bits of gnarled roots and trees carved and chipped as animal sculpture. Photographs were not allowed, which I regretted, for the pieces of sculpture were imaginative and interesting.

Outside the museum we stood on the hillside talking. In the background the hill sloped to our ger in a pasture with the village of wooden houses below and pasture, hills, and forest beyond. Black clouds above turned the sunset into a series of spotlights on our scene. We entered our vehicles again. Moments later when we stepped out of them at the ger, it was dusk. The other tents,

Drivers, Janet, Rory, the museum keeper, Patrice, and Jean-Louis

probably erected for shade, had blown down in the wind or been taken down in our absence. The wind was still too strong to erect our own tents. We took our sleeping mats and bags into the ger. The locals removed all its furniture and covered it, for rain was coming. Most of us slept in the ger, others in the vehicles. Squealing with glee and stepping on each other in the dark, we took some time to settle down, but we slept well. Laura and David's feet were at my head and Chris was next to me. We left space near the door for the handcyclists. In the dark we counted ourselves aloud for a total of twenty-two in the ger.

I awoke Wednesday to light shining under the felt and canvas wall where it met the ground near my nose. The air was fresh and clean. People began to stir inside their sleeping bags. Sounds of moving nylon fabric continued, punctuated by zippers on day bags, and air being squeezed out of self-inflatable mattresses. I put on my duty clothes and stuffed and rolled my bedding. Someone asked how we could get the top open so that we could see. "I'll do it," I replied and went outside around to the back of the ger opposite the door, where I untied the rope and hauled it until the top was open. Then I retied it, wishing I had paid attention to the original knot so

I could retie it the same way. Inside again I picked up my stuff and carried it to the vans. The ger was almost empty. I mounted my bike and rolled down the way I had come over the pasture to the road, following others to the bar for breakfast.

This morning I sat with Elly, Patrice, Jean-Louis, Joelle, and Kathy. Elly thought we were drinking coffee; I thought it was tea. Whatever it was, I drank three cups. Few of us ate tomato, cucumbers, or onion rings. Everyone took the bread covered with a spread that tasted like unsweetened yogurt. We scraped off as much of the spread as we could and when we had emptied the serving plate, I asked our translator Jomo for bread that was plain without the spread. When he returned with a full platter for us, we thoroughly enjoyed the brown, chewy, delicious bread. We continued eating the meat, rice, and potato dish. Both last night and this morning the food was exceptionally good.

When I finished eating I went outside and sat on a log talking with Laura. It was the first time she and I had had any time to chat quietly since we had come off the plane in Irkutsk. I felt comfortable with her. A psychotherapist with her own practice in New York, she had met David at a professional conference about a year before and had been smitten with him. But they had only known each other a few months before he began this ride as one of the core handcyclists. Now she was considering moving to California to be with David and she had feelings of concern. She had always loved New York and had no desire to leave. Troubled by the necessity of giving up her practice and ending many long-term relationships with patients, colleagues, friends, and family, she feared losing her identity, her professional self. She wondered whether she and David knew each other well enough for this to be other than a very big move with a considerable risk factor.

It was some time before everyone else emerged. Local speeches were at the other end of the building, so Laura and I continued talking until we were enveloped by the group again. Then we gathered our bikes and joined in a final "thank you, good-bye, creeping, creeping, let the hand cycles go first" departure.

I really liked this place and these gracious people. I wished that I could have tarried longer.

Our World Ride mobile village is like life, I thought—*no one can do everything, each of us must pick and choose though we travel the same road. We never know whether we're acting wisely, but we need to try our best.*

Down the small hill I rolled, and on the flat mile ahead I waved, nodded, occasionally shouting in Mongolian, "thank you" and "good-bye" to the children and adults watching us go by. What was behind the wooden fences and inside the wooden houses? Kathy had been inside a house or two in Russia and said they were very clean, neat, and cozy. We moved a little faster than creeping. I rolled faster, then slowed and was passed, then went ahead, dropped back, and caught up again. This made it interesting all the way to the highway.

For a time the Mongolian cyclist, Patrice, Jean-Louis, and I rode just slightly ahead of the group. The Mongolian sang a lullaby, I sang a wistful French campfire song I'd learned in French school in Switzerland over forty years ago. As we entered town we went into parade formation and slowed further. Patrice and I slid back, letting the hand cycles and core riders precede us. At the start of the Stage 9 ride we did this on cue or suggestion; now it sprang from heartfelt respect for the core riders.

Pedaling into the city, we saw the old town of Darchan near the railway station and continued south along broad boulevards toward the new town. The odd cart, vehicle, or horse sharing these broad streets did not interfere with our passage. Industry was on the out-skirts. Darchan is an autonomous municipality of about 100,000 people. Its name means *blacksmith*, reflective of its history and the Mongolian traditional expertise at metal craft.

Agnes and I were roommates in the Darchan hotel, so I took the op-portunity to get to know her better and to look for ways I could help her. The hotel and our rooms were comfortable. It was the only place in town permitted by the government to billet foreigners, who were required to pay double the Mongolian price. (The practice of charging two different prices based on nationality was not unique to Mongolia. I had run into it in Nepal and China.) Even after that short day of about fifty miles, I was very tired and rested in bed while Agnes showered. Although she could handle most zippers, buttons, and other two-handed jobs, a second hand for this or that took less time and was welcomed.

After eating and returning to the room, I showered, washed my hair and clothes, and brushed my teeth. Everything clean at one time—it felt good. We hung our clothes on the balcony and shuffled our Reebok bag contents. I had been carrying a poncho and was gradually identifying things that I could get rid of. Agnes said she could use the poncho. I was in need of more space and gave it to her.

In late afternoon we went down to the vans to clean our bikes. Agnes steadied each one while I wiped. I did the two-handed jobs, and she did the one-handed jobs. Patrice helped us put the wheels on again, a three- or four-handed job for me sometimes.

A tour of the town was planned so that we could see the rest of Darchan, but it failed to materialize. I welcomed unprogrammed time. Agnes showed me photographs of her young son, home, and friends. She had done a lot of bicycle racing even after the motorcycle accident that had immobilized her left arm. One or two of the guys had called my attention to her cycling strength. Paul, Sean, and Ronne, the racers, respected her ability.

At dinner Ken told me about being retired from his architect business. "I just closed it down before I left home." He had gotten into cycling in college with his friend Bob Davenport who still runs the Wandering Wheels tours. Ken said he wants to run tours for all sorts of people. He had also participated in the previous World T.E.A.M. Sports tour and hopes to be involved in its future events. I found myself wondering how I could connect a few of my ideas for seniors—not racers or competitors but recreational cyclists—with some of Ken's ideas. As usual, there was no more time for talk. We had to move on, out to the garden gazebo.

Staff announcements provided helpful information, such as the starting time for tomorrow and arrival plans for Ulan Bator, where dinner evenings would be hosted by the Mongolian Olympic Sports Committee and the U.S. Embassy. Also new for the staff, the incoming riders would arrive before our departure. Stage 9 and 10 participants would share rest periods and sightseeing. For the first time, the bicyclists would leave on Stage 10 before we Stage 9 riders flew away. I couldn't imagine why overlapping stage participants created nervousness, although our large group did expand. Perhaps no one wanted to admit to concern about crossing the Gobi Desert on a bicycle—next week.

Paul came up and offered to take me on the tandem tomorrow. Wow! For years I'd been wanting to try riding a tandem.

Thursday morning was a great scramble to dress, pack, and haul our bags down four flights of stairs to the vans, dash up to breakfast, expecting to gobble and go. Instead, there was no food. While we waited, Chris, Tom, and Gruffie waxed eloquent over their running tours yesterday during our rest time. Their appreciation of the Mongolian landscape stirred guilt about my lying in bed reading a book. Finally we ate. Taking the stairs two at a time I took photographs from our balcony. Then I grabbed our backpacks and scurried down again to the fast-filling parking lot.

It took another trip inside to bring the bikes out and pump tires. In addition to these necessities for ourselves, we helped with group luggage, filled water bottles, assisted the handcyclists and anyone else lagging. The inconvenience of getting the handcyclists up and down several floors in Mongolian hotels without elevators reminded them how fortunate they are in the United States where society and its facilities are learning to accommodate people with disabilities, as it again demonstrated to the rest of us the variety of routine hardships the disabled face.

I put my clean bike and wheel atop a van and started to change its seat to the tandem, but I didn't have to do that myself because the men were so quick with their allen wrenches. Paul was on vacation from the road marshal job, leaving it to Ken. Surrounded by vehicles and people from the hotel, at last we were ready to go. "Thank you, good-bye," we shouted. On Ken's count of three we began creeping out of the hotel parking lot. Paul led into a full roll down the wide empty streets of Darchan, the largest town we visited since Irkutsk, and the second largest city in Mongolia. He guided our tandem toward Mongolia's capital, Ulan Bator. I pedaled hands free and took photos with my eyes and my camera.

Our road was straight and rolling for a few miles. We sailed around a curve or two on wide boulevards, then went straight again, and into the countryside of Mongolia. From the prairie, undulating terrain stretched green to hills on the horizon; ahead, railroad and river routes wandered through a valley. It was a cloud-free day, not unusual in a country that brags about 283 sunny days per year. The tandem saddle I rode was attached to a cantilever seat post which absorbed the road shock—absolutely a marvelous ride. I kept asking Paul if I should spin my feet faster or lay on more pressure, and he always said, "No, it's just fine what you're doing." Two or three times we stopped briefly to turtle. There was no corn, wheat, bush, shrub, or stone, so we just stepped to the roadside. Mongolian poppies grew there.

Remounting our tandem, Paul suggested that I ride in front as captain. That was fine with me, but I couldn't reach the brake levers. "Don't worry," he mischievously assured me, "I'll pull the brake wires if need be." He lifted one and loosened it to snap against the frame. Even the first few moments I knew the stretch was too far and the pressure too much on my hands. It was the pain in my hands that was my unspoken motive for wanting to ride as stoker, where leaning on them was unnecessary. Already, I could feel numbness beginning in the ends of my fingers on the hand that had been injured. The carpal tunnel operation had resuscitated the nerves so my left hand had become useful again. The finger ends had recovered enough to type. But recent battering on bumpy roads was taking a toll, removing feeling until several hours after I stopped riding. I feared that one day the sense of touch just would not return to those fingers. I began to rest my left hand at every

Lookback while climbing a pass

opportunity. With Paul riding stoker, I didn't need brakes, but I couldn't take even one hand off the handlebars. I held less tightly with my left hand and tried to use the fingers more than the heel, keeping it free of weight.

Even pedaling up a long climb to the pass with its few short steep places was fun. Paul's pedaling was so strong I wasn't sure I was contributing any thrust for the bike. I kept pedaling anyway. (Several days later I was talking with Sean during dinner about that tandem ride. He told me he wasn't surprised. Didn't I know that Paul had been one of the top racers in America, including tandems?) Everyone stopped at the top of the pass. We were among the first to arrive and, as it turned out, last to leave, so that I enjoyed a wonderful chance to visit.

Two gers were perched in the pass close to where we parked the vehicles. I walked toward one of them where some women stood outside the door. As I approached they smiled; I nodded in return. The two young women wore layers of cotton of various patterns and colors. Outside the ger door an old lady sat on a bench in the sun, wearing her winter wool dress, heavy sheepskin boots, and a brimmed hat. They seemed pleased for me to take a photo. I pantomimed that I wanted to look inside. One of the girls came with me as I tried vainly to see into the dark interior from the sunny outside. She motioned to the other ger, which perhaps was where she lived, and I followed her in. The first ger appeared to contain three beds, this one contained two. All the beds I saw were single. Each was covered by a three-by-six-foot standard sleeping carpet that I recognized as similar to those I studied and marketed for the Tibetans of Nepal. I had no time to examine the knots and study the foundations.

Just as in Tibetan houses, the beds also held an assortment of pillows and rolled fabric, perhaps used as blankets. The stove was in the center with a pipe going through the top roof hole. Around the sides were runner-type rugs hung on the inside from about wainscoting height to the floor. Storage under the beds was in cardboard boxes. Near the door were a container of water and a wash pan on a crate-like box made of metal. There were foodstuffs on the other side of the door near the stove and a few standard utensils hanging over the storage. By the water container were a couple of brooms with handles of different lengths. It looked quite comfortable, especially if one's entire wardrobe required no more space than our Reebok bag.

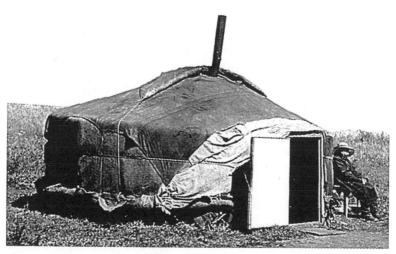

Old woman outside ger

By the time I hurried back to our group twenty or thirty yards away, people were picking up their bikes. I still needed to top up my water bottles. Paul was standing near the tandem. He suggested that I ride with Elly this section of the trip. Heaven knows what was on my face but it was not joy, though I tried to conceal my stark terror. I looked from the pass in the direction we were to travel—at least a three-mile descent. What a place to begin cycling with a new pilot. Already my hands felt worse instead of rested.

Despite my apprehension, we survived our long downhill run. The flat and slightly rolling terrain that we covered next was a great pleasure, and Elly proved to be an excellent cyclist. By the time we turned off the road into our next hotel we were laughing together.

Liza was there to hand out room numbers. She counseled us to take our bags to our rooms and come at once to lunch. A Mongolian kindly carried my bag up the steps, then I dragged it into the room. There were six beds just like those in the gers. The place had one toilet and one or perhaps two cold water taps. Liza did not consider it adequate for the night. Negotiations were underway about taking us to a pond for a swim bath. While we were waiting for lunch the staff inspected the bathing place and found it covered with green scum. They decided against that bathing option and, when the cost of our accommodations and the meals was explained, held more discussions.

Meanwhile in the room, unaware of these discussions, I changed out of my riding uniform into looser cotton clothes (shorts and a shirt) and went to the lunch building. A breeze was blowing through the village. It made sitting in the shade quite pleasant although the sun was hot. In the dining room the windows were nailed shut. The sun through the window glass created a greenhouse atmosphere suitable for tropical plants. That solar heat met kitchen heat just where we sat.

We called it sauna lunch and made jokes about the hot milk, hot tea, hot soup, hot rice, hot potatoes with hot meat, and a sort of hot mutton-burger patty. With my clean cotton shirt dripping sweat, I fled outside. Mary, Ronne, and Agnes at the same table also felt sick from the heat. Outside we recovered quickly.

I walked back to the room and lay down—glad to do nothing for a while. We were supposed to go to a river to wash, but it was expected to be muddy. After a short rest I went down to the van to get my day bag. On the way I met Liza who asked me to ask the core riders upstairs to attend a meeting to discuss whether we would stay here or move elsewhere. I told Agnes and Kathy, then lay down again. Agnes departed. Kathy dressed and left. She said the place wasn't so bad; they had stayed in worse. I told Kathy I didn't care and would just as soon stay now that we were settled. It felt good to rest. I mused about lying on exactly the same type of beds I had seen in the gers at the pass. I couldn't help thinking how much more comfortable my bed would be with a Tibetan rug under me.

Ken walked into the room. "Everyone came to the meeting except you, and we didn't want to make a decision without your vote. Everyone wants to move except you."

"When do we leave?"

"At once. The others will soon be up to bring down the bags. Are you willing to drive one of the vans? The plan is to pedal down the road another twenty-five to thirty-five miles and camp-cook our own food. We'll have spaghetti. That will cut the distance into town tomorrow from ninety-five to about sixty-five miles."

"Great idea! I'm sorry about the confusion."

"You'll drive *Tool Time*—and let's get out of here fast."

We did. I zipped my bag, and a Mongolian helped carry it down. Laura rode with me. For four hours that afternoon I drove *Tool Time* between five and ten miles per hour behind the last cyclists. Laura and I talked or enjoyed the scenery. Again they divided the cyclists into fast and slow groups. I drove behind the slow group. Sean radioed to look for camels on the left. "Camp is in a field on the right about a mile beyond the camels." A couple of times before we got there, *Black Cat* called for photo shoots. During those times the vans filled both lanes, blocking motorized traffic including the police.

A sea of green prairie grass filled the van windows. Relieving the drivers was fun and necessary because four hours of driving under ten miles per hour becomes tiresome. Steve Ackerman did not want to be pushed but lagged on the uphills that were less steep than they were long. At times *Tool Time* traveled so slowly it registered zero miles an hour.

Sean had told me that these diesel-powered vehicles were perfect for following cyclists because it didn't hurt the engine to travel so slowly as long as the driver did not ride the clutch. I had driven stick-shift cars for ages up until about ten years ago. Driving is almost as much fun for me as bicycling. Besides driving, watching our troop, and using the radio, I enjoyed listening to Laura talk about her independent therapist business and her ambivalent feelings about moving to California.

On every trip, no matter whom I was with or what I was doing or how much I enjoyed it overall, there were always a few times I wondered why in the world I was spending all day trudging through the mountains or pedaling across a desert when I could be somewhere else undisturbed by transient vexation. But then after a period of physical recovery and reflection, my perspective was restored. Appreciation and gratitude for the challenge and adventure of these experiences overrode the strain toward confor-mity and good humor under stress. Certainly my awareness about and appreciation for what the disabled face on a daily basis over-shadowed driving instead of pedaling. I knew that as soon as we arrived the wish to be there would depart along with envy of those who reached camp hours before we did. It was a struggle to keep positive thoughts in mind, that sports provide an avenue for the people of the world to come together and, of course, sports remove language barriers. In time, in retrospect, the value of these days in Russia and Mongolia, as well as how my understanding of the demands faced routinely by individuals with disabilities had expanded through the sharing of Stage 9 with such extraordinary athletes would be remembered most clearly.

Heading through a small pass we saw the camels, first mentioned by radio two and a half hours ago, on the left. Looking right, we saw our *Black Cat* van motoring down hill through a pasture to the road about half a mile ahead. By the time we reached there, Al was taking photos, and cyclists were racing down from our tents. Police and other cars driven by the Mongolians who were with us set off with no hesitation across the grass, zagging and bumping over a few hillocks and splashing through some mud. They were already climbing toward the tents. So were our cyclists. I was sitting on the roadside studying the various routes across the small pieces of stream and found a convoluted way of avoiding mud in the hope of not getting stuck. The Mongolian cars took that route. People came down to help the handcyclists, and they were now proceeding up the hill. I descended into the pasture and followed our route, bouncing over bumps, and reached the dirt and grass path uphill with no difficulty. I was directed to park a van's width distant and parallel to *Black Cat*. Al and Rick wanted to string a clothes line between our two vehicles using the roof racks for tying places. They

Leaving last camp

had some flimsy string for this purpose. "Wouldn't parachute cord be better?" I asked Al.

"A whole lot," he grinned, "like washing with soap as well as with water." "I've got a clothes line. I'll get it right away, one piece of parachute line and another of thin plastic, as well as some clothes pins," I added.

"Don't you have laundry powder too?" he teased. "No," I answered, "but I have an extra soap bar if you need it."

"Wow! That would be great, I've been out of soap for three days. Rick would be glad too, as I've been borrowing his soap and it's getting smaller because I don't give the bubbles back." Rick and Al picked a great place for a clothes line. The breeze dried our clothes before the dew came.

Strolling among the cars and tents, I picked up a piece of bread and cheese, the hot hors d'oeuvres Ken and a couple of helpers were making and serving. People were milling, talking, and drinking juice or beer. The scene was gilded by the setting sun and later lit by a crackling bonfire. Unlike the Russians, the Mongolians traveling with us pitched their tents nearby but prepared their own meals, though we shared and talked as best we could.

After eating a plate of Ken's spaghetti I went to my tent and lay down in my sleeping bag. With the dark a chill came over me. Although I had put on everything imaginable, still I was cold. I stole out into the night looking for another sleeping bag with no luck, then zipped all the windows and doors of our square tent.

But there were sounds which warmed the spirit if not the body. People were talking around the campfire, popcorn was popping, and music was playing. Camaraderie filled the air until the fire died, and utter stillness enveloped our hillside camp.

Friday I awoke at daybreak so cold I emerged wearing all the clothes I had brought except my uniform. Gruffie saved my life with a cup of her special coffee, which I sipped until it was my turn for Ken's pancakes. I piled them with syrup and fruits and nuts. Although we had cut today's ninety-five miles down to about sixty-five by adding mileage yesterday, there was no change to the planned welcome ceremony in the main square of Ulan Bator at five p.m.

Ken asked me to drive *Tool Time* this morning. Laura drove *Mash*, so we followed the cyclists again. My bike was already atop a van, so I had only to help dismantle the tents by returning the fly-tarpaulin and bungee cords to *Space Case* where they were used to hold the sleeping mats in place. After that I stowed my personal luggage, checked my film supply, and got myself ready to drive. My uniform was clean and dry, so I put it on to indicate expectations of bicycling later that day. Ronne closed down *Tool Time*'s bike shop. I was ready when the first cyclists began to roll down the pasture toward the road. Engines started, first those of the police and the Mongolian cyclist's support car. He had an incredible way of using his one leg and three prosthetic limbs to propel his bicycle at a good clip down the highway.

There were short rest stops every hour at first, then pauses at crests of small hills or passes to close any gaps among us. As the

Pause

caravan crossed gaps and valleys, I never tired of seeing the gers in the distance, sheep or horses, and kids running to the road or riding their ponies alongside the cyclists one or two at a time as we traversed their grassland.

Tom hit a pothole and tumbled off his bike. He skinned himself at hip and elbow. He was considerably shaken but rested on the roadside while Dr. John sped to him, cleaned his wounds, and made sure nothing was broken. He had time to calm down and continued pedaling rather than ride in the van. It was probably a good idea to keep himself flexible as long as he could. He pedaled all day. In the end he admitted to being tired but insisted it was fun. Tom was such a good rider he was usually at the front of the pack.

After 20 miles we stopped to lunch at a village where there was a technical school. We were each given a bowl of tea followed by a sturdy salad, soup, rice, meat, and potatoes meal. Tepid bottled drinks whose label claimed lemon flavor were standing on the table for us, too. They were wet, not carbonated, and bland. Ken asked if I would like to ride that afternoon with Patrice, stoking his tandem.

The afternoon provided a pleasant ride with Patrice, who lives near Bordeaux with his wife and two children. Riding with different people was giving me good tandem experience. I felt quite comfortable with Patrice and tried to make up for my weight by pedaling really hard on the hills, and as hard as I could sustain otherwise. I also took a lot of photos from the back of the tandem as there was no real need to hold my hands on the bars. My hands still hurt most of the time. The country was so lovely I was musing about galloping Mongols and wishing I could swap my bike for a horse—but not for long.

Ulan Bator

AFTER ASCENDING OUR LAST BIG HILL, we took a short rest stop about twenty miles from Ulan Bator. Drivers and cyclists changed places here in the pass. Tandems went up on van tops as their riders took to driving or single bikes. Jean-Louis rejoined Patrice, and I took down my Fuji Touring Series green bike for a last ride, one they said had to be fast. "It is all downhill now," they said, "and that isn't a joke."

Fast we did go. It was great fun zipping along the first ten miles in about a half-hour. The road, while still providing a bit of gravity assistance, appeared flat. Cooling towers for the power plant flashed by. We slowed over railroad tracks. The Tuul River flowed beyond a predominantly industrial area on the outskirts of Ulan Bator where we passed apartment buildings. Suddenly I heard the order, "Stop!" There was a crash. We halted carefully to prevent being rear-ended or running into someone else.

I put my bike down and walked a few yards back to where a crowd was gathering. The axle on Steve's hand cycle had broken, throwing him onto the pavement. He was quite shaken and had a bad road rash scrape over his right elbow. Everyone waited patiently. I did not go any closer. Because Al didn't seem to be around, I took a few photos of the broken axle and Steve as Dr. John cleaned and disinfected his elbow. By the time the doctor completed his examination of Steve, Ronne had repaired the hand cycle and together they helped Steve get back in it. He insisted on riding. There was a shout, "Get ready to creep," a pause, then

Peter at the ceremony in Ulan Bator

"creeping." Soon we accelerated to rolling and were moving as fast as before. I had to focus on my track rather than the buildings or people.

The police leading and those behind us turned on their sirens. We began yelling hellos in Mongolian, *sain baina yu,* as people collected along the way, waving and watching as we ran every intersection, assisted by the police. At two minutes before five in the evening, we entered the square. The crowd parted, and we pedaled

Boy in U.S. flag shorts

to the statue. People yelled and clapped. We hopped off our bicycles in front of a few people standing by a microphone. There were welcome banners. Former communists, we observed over the past two weeks, were magnificent at producing and hanging banners! Our advance team was there, Liza and Terry along with Jomo the interpreter.

We were welcomed by speeches from the Ministry of Health people and the local Olympic Committee. A number of spectators had obvious disabilities. I was touched that they had come here to see us. A man played an accordion, a woman sang. Everyone took photos. TV cameras whirred. Western tourists were watching us too. Some of them were gray-heads like me, others looked like backpackers or students. One little boy in the front row had an Asian face and wore shorts that resembled the American flag.

Representatives from the American Embassy were present, along with a few other professional-looking Westerners.

The center of each city we entered in Siberia and Mongolia included a big open place marked by a memorial statue. Here in Ulan Bator the founder of the new Mongolian state, Suchbaatar, sat on his horse in bronze. I thought this practice not unlike colonial Savannah, constructed around a series of squares, and the many other American towns with a center marked by the courthouse building and its park. Though not all square-shaped, the public spaces we had seen on our bicycle tour were used for ceremonial gatherings, parades, and rallies. I wondered whether one could estimate the population by the size of the main public square. This square was so large it dwarfed our few hundred people clustered around the statue.

In Suchbaatar Square, Ulan Bator: David, Laura, and Tom

Suchbaatar Square in Ulan Bator was indeed a capital square. Surely it was the biggest central public area we had entered. The statue provided a historic symbol of the foundation of modern Mongolia as well as a place from which to measure kilometers to the next town square. Facing south, I realized the city was built on an alluvial plane that slanted slightly toward a ring of mountains. Turning around, I had an unrestricted view another range. We were in an alpine valley. The buildings we had passed appeared central European communist in architectural style; the boulevards were four to six lanes wide. Around the square, buildings seemed influenced by the Tibetan slanting walls and window forms and bore Chinese-style roofs with turned-up edges to keep evil spirits out by causing them to slide back up into the air. Other roofs seemed to imitate tent shapes. These imposing buildings of stone made the square feel like a miniature valley within its vast circle of mountains. A place of grandeur and a fitting end to Stage 9. After the formalities, our group congratulated each other with hugs and handshakes.

The ten days of cycling we had experienced were a small part of the whole World Ride mid-March to mid-November. The core group was just beyond the half-way point of the entire ride. They had a long way to go, and the challenge of crossing the Gobi desert loomed ahead for them.

The hoopla over, we began picking up our bicycles, taking a few more photos and preparing to pedal only a few blocks to our hotel. Our bicycles would be parked there. We would have to use our feet. This was a dream city to explore by bicycle, for the streets were wide, and traffic was sparse.

Walking my bike past some of the spectators, I caught sight of a man in a wheelchair on the front row of standing people. His chair was moved by cranking levers, and the whole metal frame of the chair was painted a brilliant blue. Rory, behind me, steered his hand cycle toward the man, who cranked his chair out a few feet from the crowd. Neither able to speak the other's language, these two men beamed with smiles and nods of empathy as they shook hands. I snapped their photo, for their encounter symbolized our purpose here.

We heard the police cars begin to move. We had shouted our official thanks and farewells but individually we said "thank you, good-bye" again and again as we mounted our bicycles. We began creeping as people moved off on foot. After turning two corners I dismounted for the last time as a World T.E.A.M. stage rider. We pushed our bikes into the hotel, down a hall into a storage room. In a few days they would leave on Stage 10.

Mongolian greets Rory McCarthy

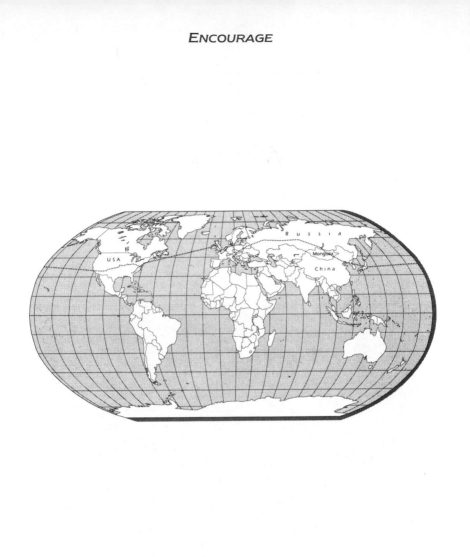

Windup

Chris Noonan

ON THIS PLATEAU Ulan Bator originated in the 1ˢᵗ century as the home of a living Buddha. Its first name translated as "great camp." In 1911, when Mongolia proclaimed its independence from China and set up a theocratic government, the city was renamed "capital camp," known in the west as Urga. Mongolia's predominant religion remains Tibetan Buddhist Lamaism. In 1924 it became Ulan Bator.

Mongolia's sprawling capital city has a population of over 600,000. There's plenty of open space—wide boulevards, squares, parks, and Soviet monuments. To us it had the look and feel of the 1950s, from the colonnaded buildings to vintage Soviet cars and ancient German motorcycles with sidecars.

The city center is dominated by Soviet-style high-rise apartment blocks, but much of the population lives in ger suburbs. These city gers are enclosed by fences that protect them from fierce wind in the spring. At 5,000 feet altitude, the city sprawls along the banks of the Tuul River.

Our first morning, Sunday, August 28, in Ulan Bator the bathroom flooded. It was tiled up about four feet. Between the toilet and wash basin was a drain, but the floor slanted so that with each shower an inch-deep lake appeared near the sill to the hall. Long after showers our lake remained. We soon developed a habit of stepping over it. The shower's hose twitched erratically spraying towels as well as the person. Water was plentiful and hot except for the first day when the city's hot-water facility was not working. We were told that water for Ulan Bator was heated in a Soviet-built, coal-burning system, then piped throughout the buildings. Some pipes are visible along the road to the airport. Our shower flowed so hot we often had to add cold water to keep from burning ourselves. Our drinking water came from boilers in the kitchen, but we procured it from the thermal jugs that kept it hot all day in our vans.

Outside the door to the dining room, we gathered for breakfast at seven-thirty in the morning. Finally a man from the desk came to unlock the door. Despite the table's not being set, we seated ourselves and waited while several staff members with worried faces came and went from the kitchen. The cook had not come to work—and he held all the keys. Prepaid or not, there would be no breakfast. We left. At our invitation, Patrice and Jean-Louis came to our living room for peanut butter and jelly crackers. We drank the sodas that I stashed the night before, but my water bottles were empty. Paul came in while we were eating, looking for something to drink. I assured him that the American Embassy would offer us coffee.

We boarded our buses without a chance to get water from the vans. Maybe the coolers were empty. It was a thirsty morning. Upon entering the embassy foyer we discovered chairs set up for us. I saw no sign of liquid nor did I smell coffee. Ambassador Johnson came out to greet us. He spoke briefly about Mongolia, then answered our questions concerning his background, how many people worked at the embassy, and what they did. He politely ignored our foot shuffling, whispering, and general inattention. He confirmed our observation that there were very few people working there. I never saw any U.S. Marine guards, nor did he mention them. The Johnsons also lived in the embassy. Ambassador Johnson had served previously in both Russia and China and had learned both languages. He had learned Mongolian prior to his arrival here and continued his study of it. A recital of his past duties and ranks quieted the cyclists a bit, indicating a degree of respect. I wondered whether they realized how they must appear to a diplomat accustomed to courtesy, protocol, and subtlety.

Maybe it was only in my mind and I unfairly credited the same feelings to others, but the highlight of the visit came when the ambassador introduced his wife, who offered a container of homemade cookies and Cokes to our group. Paul thanked the ambassador and his wife for our visit, and Tore Naerland, who had joined us from Norway, presented the ambassador with a bell from the Olympic Games there. I had heard about Tore, who rode with the group in Europe on the back of a tandem. He has about five percent of his eyesight and has made a career of encouraging the disabled all over the world. Later, he gave me a copy of his account of these travels, published by the former Communist regime in Russia.

Somewhere toward the end of our visit, in response to a question about embassy life, the ambassador offered to show us the rest of the embassy. There was no response, for perhaps his soft-spoken comment had been missed amongst the cookie-munching, Coke can tops popping, and general shuffling. After Tore's presentation we rose and many of us shook the ambassador's hand, had photos taken with him, then without a full cry "1, 2, farewell," began creeping out the door on foot. He escorted us to the gate still conversing with individuals. Ambassador Johnson impressed me as a splendid gentleman and, no doubt, an excellent diplomat, a real professional—and I had seen a lot of them in years past, both political appointees and career officers.

By bus we continued our journey to the Ministry of Health and Education where we were met with the accustomed fanfare. We followed our hosts down corridors and up flights of steps, hauling the handcyclists in their wheel chairs up to the fourth-floor conference room. The room was quite large, wood paneled, equipped with microphones, and held a large horseshoe-shaped conference table that accommodated all of us.

We were served cookies, candies, and lemon soda or beer while watching raw footage of our trip, taken by the Mongolian TV people, from the border toward Ulan Bator. When the video was turned off, a few speeches of welcome were delivered. Then a video tape was shown about the life of the Mongolian cyclist who accompanied us. He had lost both arms and a leg in an electrical fire accident. There were scenes of his various therapies, in-bed exercises, walking exercises, and so on. His wife left him. He married anew and began swimming, cycling, and other sports to strengthen his body so that he could function with the prosthetic arms and leg that we had observed with awe as he pedaled with us from the border to the capital city. He planned to ride with Stage 10 as well. Tended by his current wife and others in a car, he would continue to the Chinese border. The video provided background information that helped us understand how he became a respected person in Mongolia. He is a splendid representative of and example for disabled people everywhere. More speeches were translated. We thanked our hosts and began our descent down the stairs.

Our bus then headed for the lamasery. It recently reopened to the practice of Buddhism. The place reminded me of Tibetan and Nepali Buddhist temples. An exception were the table-like structures in the courtyard, with two legs shorter than the other pair, and both low to the ground. After thinking about it for a while I decided they must have been built originally for prostrating oneself during prayer in the old custom. I had never seen such structures in a temple nor seen photos of them anywhere. I asked our English-speaking guide what they were. She replied, "For prayer, but the young people do not do that any more."

Monks were chanting inside the temple, where photos were not allowed. I went inside the door and glanced around. The place was crowded with monks of all ages. They sat on good wool carpets with traditional designs. But I dislike hypnotic chanting, and the smell of incense and butter. Fresh air beckoned me into the courtyard where we could still hear the chanting, bells, and horns. I sat in the sun and watched people, most of whom were watching us.

Workers high on scaffolds were restoring this treasure-trove

Prosthetic arms of the Mongolian cyclist

tourist attraction temple complex. Allowed to fall into disrepair, the monastery was not destroyed during the communist regime. It remained in service, but the head monk was a KGB member undercover. Upon Mongolian independence, he retired and was replaced by a lama.

Ambling back toward our bus, several of us looked at drawings and prints for sale. I spotted a couple of silk scarves blowing in the wind that appeared to be hand painted in a freehand, fluid style in shades of blue and green. They depicted gers, ponies, and people much like those I had seen from my bicycle. I headed that way. A young girl asked in English if she could show me something. When her list reached, "scarf?" I nodded. She told me the price, $19, which seemed reasonable, and continued to speak, "handpainted, all silk; I painted them myself. My brother does the drawings." I felt one of the scarves and offered fifteen dollars. She regarded me intently then said, "yes." We made our transaction, and I tucked the scarf away. I had no idea of local prices, but the silk weighed nothing.

After lunch, I joined a group going shopping. Staff members were busy confirming our flights home and with preparations to meet the Stage 10 people. With Jomo as translator, several of us wandered through the State Department Store, the Duty Free Shop and a hotel shop, as well as a book store for school kids. The stores reminded me of the state stores I had visited in Central Europe and China. There were departments for everything from food and clothing to housewares. I was not looking for anything yet bought six postcards and a bag of popcorn. Others selected gifts for their spouses and children. Mongolian hats were popular, as were small items of wood, maps, drawings, and tourist items, including toys and jewelry.

On returning to the hotel, Mary and I showered in water that was too hot. I nearly scalded my head but emerged with clean hair. We dressed in the best we could pull out of our bags, then proceeded by bus to the Ger Palace. It is the largest ger in the world we were informed. It took two years to build and has been in use now for three years for public and state functions as well as weddings. The hole in the roof is the size of a normal ger. As usual, the wooden floor is covered by rugs. We were not sure whether it was a stand-up dinner at which we finally sat down or a sit-down meal during which about half the time we stood. There were drinks of all sorts, including wines and brandy, as well as fruit drinks and colas. Fresh fruits, slices of peach, apple, and orange were welcome, for these items had been rare since coming into Mongolia.

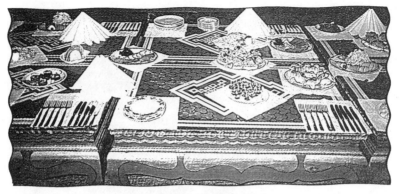

Banquet table in the Ger Palace

When I spoke with Ambassador Johnson, he assured me Stage 10 would have little trouble pedaling the dirt road through the Gobi Desert to China—unless it rained.

We were interrupted by the arrival of the Stage 10 riders who had just landed. Ron Bell and his friends Bob Gries and Bruce Sherman from Cleveland had participated together in the Race Across America about three weeks ago. Like any party we shifted groups and continued talking as fast as we could among ourselves and the guests. Happily satisfied by food, drink, and company we eventually straggled to our bus and arrived at our hotel.

More Stage 10 arrivals came during the night or early morning. We assembled Monday as guests of Peter, a board member and a founder of World Team Sports, for breakfast at the Hotel Ulan Bator some blocks down the street. An invigorating walk brought us to a splendid buffet. We helped ourselves repeatedly. Not only coffee and tea, but hot chocolate was available. We felt like royalty thanks to Peter's arrangements.

During breakfast we stood and introduced ourselves in turn. We of Stage 9 conveyed our envy at not going on with them. We also expressed our joy, pride, and sense of having benefited ourselves while hoping to have stimulated others during our participation in World Ride.

Some of us echoed Peter's speech when we left Russia: "People are lonely because they have been building walls instead of bridges.

Kiosk in Ulan Bator

The time when people constructed walls is gone. You are among the first who, instead of walls, build bridges between our nations."

Peter Kiernan closed the session by commenting on his participation in Stage 9 saying, "It is truly a magical event, one that far transcends issues of disability, or for that matter, sports or cycling."

While clapping our agreement we gave Peter a spontaneous shouted, "thank you," in Mongolian of course. Then we wandered around the dining room speaking to each other, greeting the newcomers and finally, a few at a time, walking back to the hotel, still chatting.

A bus took us to the Natural History Museum. We circulated through the galleries, returning to the kiosks which sold local art and crafts as well as modern cashmere sweaters. Of course we looked at the dinosaur bones and other exhibits of geology, flora, fauna, and ethnographics too, but buying required more time. I bought a black leather handbag that unzipped into a backpack.

For lunch the bus took us to the Genghis Khan Hotel, an enormous pile of glass and modern architecture. It was like walking around in an unfinished sculpture. We found the elevator that worked and sped to the top floor. There were no guests. We walked through a bar that awaited furniture and bottles. Suffering from lack of funds and supplies, the Genghis Khan Hotel construction was years overdue for completion. The roof level dining room, where our banquet table for sixty to seventy people was set, was the only place in use.

We enjoyed a splendid view of the Tuul River and the Ger Palace, where we dined last night, as well as Ulan Bator in its mountain-walled valley. At home this hotel would have cost several hundred dollars a day, and our lunch would have been pricey. Here, food was inexpensive. Nevertheless, it was a smashingly successful meal. The tasty food was artisticly arranged and served; bonding occurred between Stage 9 and Stage 10 participants, between staff and johnny-come-latelies, between core riders who by this time must have been old hands at fancy banquets, and our local hosts, the Department of Health and the Olympic Committee. It was definitely a lunch to remember.

Stage 10 bicycle fitting was held that afternoon in our hotel parking lot. I stood around for some time watching as people came. Among the arrivals was Julie Milstien, an American working in Geneva with the World Health Organization in the Global Programme for Vaccines and Immunization. She was the only new woman cyclist. Ronne had adjusted the bike I used to fit her. Peter introduced his friend Ann from Atlanta who would be a van driver.

None of us could miss the tall Tim Paul. We could see him but he couldn't observe us for he is blind. He came to stoke a tandem. Tim was having trouble recognizing people, for he had not yet heard our voices often enough to remember them. Getting around in these strange places required as much help for him as Jean-Louis. (Did you ever drop a pen on the floor in the dark and try to find it without turning on a light? I just couldn't imagine how this trip was perceived by Tim and Jean-Louis.)

Thus, I chanced to learn something of these new Stage 10 ped-alers. Mostly I watched the kids, speaking to keep them away from the bicycles and the cars, itself a full-time job. I pumped a few tires

but otherwise enjoyed being in the
sun and watching Stage 10 people
prepare themselves for their adventure. Ronne did most of the bike
fitting. Sean changed wheel after
wheel from road slick treads to tires
with more tread and a wider base for
off-road stability, because we knew
that beyond the city pavement ran
only about thirty miles or less. We
had heard repeatedly that the busiest
road in Mongolia is the one we just
traveled. To the south were few
people, much less traffic, dirt roads,
and fewer villages. Seldom had we
seen more than three or four a day.

Jean-Louis Gouzy

I continued with these activities longer than intended because
Mary had taken the room key. She and Patrice had gone to buy
beer, for we had invited people to our "suite" this evening. At first
Mary and I had thought everyone had a living room with a fridge as
well as a bedroom and bath off the entry. Not so. We had received
spacious accommodations. Beer procurement required visits to two
or three shops and triple the expected time.

Back in the room we stowed the beer in the fridge, then began to
reshuffle the contents of our bags. This time I emptied everything
out of my bag and put back only those items I needed. Food, note-
books, pens, film, and tissue packets were gathered up and taken to
Kathy, Agnes, and Elly who were delighted by the resupply.

The Mongolian Olympic Committee representatives had
invited us to dinner. We were driven in two buses to a hall near a
sports stadium.

The dinner was lengthy. Sitting next to Sean, I noticed that he
was filling the pauses by reading something concealed under his
napkin. When I asked him what it was, he produced a copy of Lao
Tzu's *Tao Te Ching*. I promised to send him the Isabella Mears

translation, if possible, though out of print, for I feel it more clear. The meal was excellent, as was the entertainment. I sat across from Jean-Louis, Mary, Patrice, and John, but next to Michael who had just come and remained quite silent.

Entertainers were singers, dancers, and musicians much like the ones we had seen in Ulan-Ude, especially the contortionists. This time there was a single woman, then later a pair of them, who bent themselves into positions the human body was never intended to assume. Even some of the men agreed that the most interesting performance was by a man who sang a single note with different, slightly

Contortionists

buzzing string-like variations. We asked him to sing over and over. He gave a magnificent performance (of overtone singing), far beyond anything I had ever heard a human voice achieve. A week or so later, *The Washington Post* carried an article about Mrs. Clinton's visit to Mongolia. It mentioned "a 13-year-old contortionist who bent over backward, put her head between her legs from behind and balanced herself on her chin, and a man who sang a single note with different, slightly buzzing, string-like variations; and some tunes on a horse fiddle." If they were not the same individuals, they were demonstrating the same skills.

I read about a singer who made stunning noises with his bass voice. The sound filled the whole Ger Palace and could be heard for miles, a song technique used traditionally as a signal. Thus old Mongolia blends with modern Mongolia in music and entertainment.

The Mongolian cyclist and his family were there, as were the Mongolian bicycle racers who had ridden out to meet and accompany us back to the capital. So were the other dignitaries and our translator Jomo. After about ten o'clock, we offered individual good-byes whether or not we could speak a mutual language, for we felt and appreciated the outpouring of hospitality and tried to show that to them by smiling, nodding, shaking hands, and saying *thank you* in Mongolian. Then we climbed into the buses. The cool night air was welcome.

Mostly Stage 9 people convened in our party room for beer with core riders and staff. We all talked at once, recalling memories and stories of our time together. Unable to stay awake any longer, I went to bed, lulled by the voices of comrades.

Breakfast in our hotel Tuesday was at the usual table. We were beginning to feel at home there. Stage 10 people and staff, however, came and went. Finally, I rose to my feet, having sat there chatting, and followed Ken and several guys carrying empty water jugs to the kitchen. I had seen neither this process nor the kitchen. Boiled water, still quite hot, was run from the boiler spigot into our coolers, at first just enough to rinse them. This first amount was poured out and the coolers were filled and topped before being carried to the vans. Ken wanted every container filled, for getting water in more sparsely populated southern Mongolia would not be so easy as it had been for us in the north. There were few if any towns large enough to have institutional kitchens. I followed them out to the sunny parking lot to photograph the Stage 10 departure. I stood watching. I really did want to go with them. Without me to chase them, the kids were all over our bikes and vehicles. Well, this was Stage 10's day now. Al's camera and all the others were turned away from us—now spectators.

I walked out to the street and stood by the police cars and the Mongolian cyclist's family car. Paul, standing over his bike, was talking on the radio. We joined in their thank you, good-bye, shouts and stood waving as they began creeping into the street. I clicked off a few photos, and they were gone.

In Ken's van I rode to the State Department Store with Mary, Ken, Dr. John, Peter, and Jomo. The men bought their family gifts;

*Last photo — 1ˢᵗ row: Mary, Elly, Gruffie, Janet; 2ⁿᵈ row: Tom, Dr. John,
Laura, Jean-Louis, Joelle, Eliza, Peter, Patrice; 3ʳᵈ row: Chris and Terry*

I a couple of spoons and a bowl of carved wood, for no reason except they were small and I liked them. Ken agreed that I could come along with him, Dr. John, Peter, and Jomo to buy more food for the Stage 10 ride. We entered the food shops where cases of water and juice, jars of peanut butter and jelly, pasta, and other staples were purchased for their camping meals.

At another place he bought cases and cases of Evian spring water imported from France. At a dollar a liter, it was worth every cent. The bottles were plastic; the weight was the water. Ken knew they would need as much water as the vehicles could carry.

Our last stop was the local market I had not found previously; it thrilled me to enter. (I cannot resist a market.) We carried to the van four dozen eggs, six kilos of frozen chicken parts (legs) from the U.S., carrots, onions, zucchini, and potatoes that Ken intended to prepare with the chicken for that night's dinner.

There was no time to spare, for Ken had to catch up with the group in time to provide their lunch. Nevertheless, he made one more stop for cases of individual cans of apple juice and pineapple juice, as well as cornflakes and instant oatmeal. Now he had everything except the bread. That he would obtain on the way out of town. The vans were stacked to the ceiling; the bread would replace one of us.

We met *Black Cat*, headed for the airport to try to find the rest of a hand cycle that had not arrived the day before and the new director/producer who would travel with Al. Ken returned to the hotel to drop off Stage 9 people; Peter and I rode with our legs folded on top of cases of juice and water. We got out, and he picked up Terry who was continuing with Stage 10.

Al Eastman

Stage 9 was over. I spent the rest of the afternoon reading in bed and repacking my stuff, and thinking. Any one street or building in Ulan Bator was not interesting at first glance yet there is a feel, an openness, a spaciousness to the town, and an overall pleasantness about the place. I liked Mongolia.

If all went well, I would be home in two days. Our staff put us all on the weekly plane from Ulan Bator to Moscow, where Patrice and Jean-Louis transferred airports and planes to continue to France. Liza booked us into the best food buffet of our trip at our Moscow Novotel. So much had happened during these past two weeks that they seemed more like two years. We'd been so busy or tired that now we spent the evening in a flood of talk, shared stories, and jokes, an outpouring interrupted by good-byes to Bob and Gruffie, who would be catching a pre-dawn plane. That left eleven of us for the New York plane a few hours later.

Over clattering baggage carousels in New York our thank yous and good-byes, accompanied by hugs rather than shouts, ended with, "See you in Washington," where the World Ride would end.

A number of us intended to join one or more of the last three stages—the ride across America—or at minimum the last day entry into Washington, D.C.

No one mentioned what we all felt, that this experience would influence the rest of our lives. Sharing the road with World Ride '95 had opened physical, emotional, and mental windows on the richness and value of living.

Spasiba. Thank you. Bayartai. Good-bye.

Jane Schnell

Stages of AXA World Ride '95

STAGE 1
The New South
Atlanta, GA, to Washington, DC
767 miles, March 17–27

STAGE 2
The Eastern Corridor to New England
Washington, DC, to Boston, MA
510 miles, March 28–April 8

STAGE 3
The Royal Route to France
Shannon, Ireland, to Paris, France
709 miles, April 9–26

STAGE 4
The Northern Route to Vienna
Paris, France, to Vienna, Austria
1,348 miles, April 27–May 21

STAGE 5
Eastern Europe to Russia
Vienna, Austria, to Moscow, RF*
1,257 miles, May 22–June 15

STAGE 6
Across the Ural Mountains
Moscow, RF, to Celjabinsk, RF
1,108 miles, June 26–July 4

STAGE 7
The Heart of Siberia
Celjabinsk, RF, to Novosibirsk, RF
1,028 miles, July 5–23

STAGE 8
The Mysterious Altai Mountains
Novosibirsk, RF, to Irkutsk, RF
1,143 miles, July 24–August 15

STAGE 9
The Steppes of Mongolia
Irkutsk, RF, to Ulan Bator, Mongolia
563 miles, August 16–27

STAGE 10
Mongolia South to China
Ulan Bator, Mongolia, to Beijing, China
943 miles, August 28–September 15

STAGE 11
Historical Japan
Hiroshima to Tokyo, Japan
325 miles, September 16–28

STAGE 12
The Old West
Los Angeles, CA, to Santa Fe, NM
993 miles, September 29–October 12

STAGE 13
The Great Plains
Santa Fe, NM, to St. Louis, MO
1,325 miles, October 13–30

STAGE 14
The Heartland to Washington, DC
St. Louis, MO, to Washington, DC
1,007 miles, October 31–November 18

*Russian Federation

Background

About World T.E.A.M. Sports

FOUNDED IN 1993 by Jim Benson, World T.E.A.M. (The Exceptional Athlete Matters) Sports is a national sports charity committed to encouraging, promoting, and developing opportunities for persons with disabilities in lifetime sports and recreation activities. World T.E.A.M. Sports is dedicated to creating avenues for all persons to enjoy sports, thus providing the most level playing field where everyone gains and there is an atmosphere of collective cooperation.

AXA World Ride '95, the first official worldwide event sponsored by World T.E.A.M. Sports, was an around-the-world, eight-month cycling challenge covering 13,000 miles. Over 200 able-bodied and disabled cyclists participated, including six athletes (5 with disabilities) who completed the entire route. AXA World Ride '95 served to showcase the abilities of all persons and demonstrate that athletic victory rests on a delicate balance of personal sacrifice, perseverance, courage, and a limitless desire to build a team of exceptional members.

World Ride '95 Fast Facts

♦ Disabled and able-bodied athletes pedaled around the globe in an eight-month challenge ride.

♦ The ride began on March 17, 1995, in Atlanta, Georgia, and ended on November 18, 1995, in Washington, D.C.

♦ The ride was divided into fourteen stages (each with twenty-five to thirty-five cyclists) and covered 13,026 miles. Sixteen countries were visited, including, in chronological order, the United States, Ireland, United Kingdom, France, Belgium, Netherlands, Germany, Czech Republic, Austria, Poland,

Belarus, Kazakhstan, Siberia, Russian Federation, Mongolia, Peoples Republic of China, Japan, and the United States.

◆ Seven core cyclists, six disabled, began the journey. More than 225 able-bodied and disabled cyclists joined the core riders at various locations throughout the world as stage participants.

◆ Major celebratory event days occurred during the ride.

◆ Greg LeMond, three-time champion of the Tour de France, served as Honorary Chairman for AXA World Ride '95. He participated in various stages.

◆ The AXA Group, the world's fourth largest insurance company, was the title sponsor for World Ride '95

◆ Presenting sponsors included The Equitable Life Assurance Society, Reebok International, Ernst & Young, and Olsten Staffing Services.

◆ World Ride '95 was organized by World T.E.A.M. (The Exceptional Athlete Matters) Sports, a non-profit group dedicated to promoting and developing opportunities for persons with disabilities to participate in lifetime sports activities.

World T.E.A.M. Sports (WTS) Facts

◆ World Team Sports is based in Charlotte, North Carolina.

◆ WTS is working with the Dennis Byrd Foundation to develop a prototype recreational camp for disabled young people.

◆ WTS sponsors amateur sports teams which form training and recreational partnerships with disabled athletes.

◆ WTS works with existing sports organizations dedicated to furthering the cause of disabled athletes by integrating these individuals into the athletic community.

◆ WTS along with the 1996 Atlanta Paralympic Organizing Committee coordinates the T.E.A.M. Mates program which unites professional athletes with elite-level disabled athletes in promotion campaigns for non-profit organizations.

World T.E.A.M. Sports is deep into its next challenges and plans. To receive their newsletter or participate, contact them at Suite 101, 2108 South Blvd., Charlotte, NC 28203, Tele. (704) 370-6070; Fax (704) 370-7750.

The Disabled Community

THE AMERICANS WITH DISABILITIES ACT (ADA) was signed on July 26, 1990, by President Bush.

Under the ADA an individual is disabled if that individual has a physical or mental impairment that substantially limits a major life activity; has a record of such an impairment; or regarded as having such an impairment.

◆ The most common disabilities are orthopedic (amputations), arthritis, heart disease, visual impairments, spinal disk disorders, asthma, nervous disorders, and mental disorders.

◆ The Bureau of Census reported in 1992:

   ◆ There are 48.9 million people with disabilities in the United States.

   ◆ There are over 500 million people with disabilities in the world.

   ◆ The buying power of people with disabilities in the United States alone is $700 billion.

◆ The 1994 Harris Survey reports:

   ◆ Only 47% of people with disabilities believe that others treat them as equals as opposed to feeling sorry for them or being embarrassed.

   ◆ Only 35% of adults with disabilities are satisfied with their lives in general, compared to 55% of people without disabilities.

Stage 9

The Steppes of Mongolia

Irkutsk, Russian Federation (Siberia) to Ulan Bator, Mongolia

563 miles.

August 16–27, 1995

Departure

August 13–15:   New York to Moscow to Irkutsk

Overnight stops during Stage 9

August 15:   Irkutsk–Hotel Intourist
August 16:   Truck Stop motel
August 17:   Lake Baikal bluff camp
August 18:   Orphanage village
August 19:   Ulan-Ude hotel
August 20:   Riverside camp
August 21:   Suchbaatar, Mongolia, hotel
August 22:   Ger camp
August 23:   Darchan hotel
August 24:   Pasture camp
August 25:   Ulan Bator hotel
August 26:   Ulan Bator hotel
August 27:   Ulan Bator hotel
August 28:   Ulan Bator hotel

Return

August 29–30:   Ulan Bator to Moscow to Washington

BIOGRAPHIES reprint information received from World T.E.A.M. Sports. They have been updated and corrected whenever possible.

The People of Stage 9

Core is a term for people who were along for the entire World Ride. *Participant* indicates people along for one or more stages. It also includes day riders or anyone who participated in the ride no matter how long the duration. A few participants are not listed here because they joined for a day or a few hours; their full names were unknown to the author.

Core Riders

Steve Ackerman	handcyclist
David Cornelsen	handcyclist
Ronne Irvine	prosthetic foot—standard bicycle
Agnes Kearon	controls single bike with one arm
Rory McCarthy	handcyclist
Kathryn Rosica	standard bicycle

Core Staff

Paul Curley	road chief
Sean Carithers	road leader, assistant mechanic
Ken Snelling	provisions
Ronne Irvine	mechanic
Al Eastman	photographer

Core Riders

Steve Ackerman—Paralyzed from the hips down since an automobile accident in 1987, Steve skis, swims, and cycles. He was the first person to complete the 400-mile Ride the Rockies by arm power. He has done it four times! A sales representative for Freedom Rider Hand Cycle Corporation, he promotes hand cycling and works to introduce injured people to sports. Steve lives in Colorado.

David Cornelsen—A car accident in 1987 left David paralyzed from the hips down. He has set several world records for hand cycling, has won a number of championships and was chosen Bicyclist of the Year in 1991 by *Bicycling Magazine*. In the Race Across America, he traveled 2,969 miles in 18 days, 16 hours and 52 minutes. David works for Research Medical, for Presbyterian Community Hospital, and for Orthopedic Products Corporation. He holds a PhD in social work and a Masters in religion. David lives in California. David and Laura married since the ride.

Ronne Irvine—Ronne lost his left foot and two fingers on the right hand in a car accident in 1975. His cycling victories include many national and international championships and a tenth place in the Barcelona Paralympics. Ronne not only rides, he also serves as team mechanic for the events in which he participates (including AXA World Ride '95). He works as service manager for The Bicycle Exchange in Reston, Virginia.

Agnes Kearnon—It wasn't until after the motorcycle accident in 1981 which cost her the use of her left arm that Agnes began to take an interest in sports and to excel in cycling. She has done a lot of racing and has attended the United States Sports Team development camp at the U.S. Olympic Training Center in Colorado Springs, Colorado. Agnes lives in Ballston Spa, New York, where she is a medical records technician at the Center for the Disabled.

Rory McCarthy—With muscular atrophy in his legs, Rory can walk with crutches. He has been handcycling since 1982 and has logged literally thousands of miles all over the United States as well as in England, Wales, and China. Rory is a project engineer for Enterprise Engineering, Inc., in West Bath, Maine. He also works with groups in his hometown to promote sports for the disabled.

Kathryn Rosica—The only able-bodied core rider, Kathy has spent her life since childhood in activities whose goal is to integrate people of differing abilities into competitive events. A graduate of Northeastern University, Kathy works as a toxicologist for the

Chemical Manufacturers Association in Washington, D.C. She lives in Falls Church, Virginia.

Core Staff

Paul Curley—Paul has been riding bicycles for 35 years and racing for 20 years. Eleven times national champion, he also holds the National Masters Tandem road race title. Licensed as a coach by the US Cycling Federation, Paul runs a personal training business. As Operations Director of the World Ride '95, he oversaw the day-to-day operation of the entire ride.

Sean Carithers—Sean is a racing cyclist and a staff member of World T.E.A.M. Sports and of AXA World Ride '95 (which he helped plan).

Ken Snelling—Ken rides his bicycle over two thousand miles a year. But that's not all! He has served the National Ski Patrol as instructor for visually impaired skiers; he has led many mountain climbing and kayaking expeditions. He also runs, and completed the 1992 New York City Marathon. Ken has established his own architecture practice in Jacksonville, Oregon, where he lives with his wife and three children. He is a core team leader with World T.E.A.M. Sports.

Stage 9 Participants

James M. Benson—Jim Benson of Greenwich, Connecticut, is a founder-director of World T.E.A.M. (The Exceptional Athlete Matters) Sports, an organization dedicated to providing opportunities through sports for people with both mental and physical disabilities. He is President and CEO of Equitable Life. Mr. Benson has been active in the life insurance industry for more than 25 years. He is also active in industry and community organizations, serving on the boards of the Life Underwriting Training Council, the California Special Olympics, the Joffrey Ballet, and the African Wildlife Foundation.

Steve Whisnant—Steve co-founded World T.E.A.M. Sports in 1993 after fifteen years in non-profit management. Steve, who has extensive experience in fund raising, sports development, and administration, is responsible for the entire day-to-day operations of World T.E.A.M. Sports. In 1988 Steve was awarded a Lyndhurst Prize for his work in community service. He and his wife live in Charlotte, North Carolina.

Dr. John Campbell—John lives in Greensboro, North Carolina, and is an infectious diseases specialist at Moses Cone Hospital. He was the team doctor on Stage 9.

Gruffie Clough—Gruffie lives in Denver, Colorado, where she runs her own business as an organizational development consultant. She has worked with Outward Bound for 20 years as a course director and instructor. She has lived and worked in Africa for over 10 years. Gruffie enjoys kayaking, mountaineering and cycling all over the world. She has been helping World Ride core riders with conflict management and team building. Her husband Robert Roark rode a hand cycle on Stage Nine.

Terry Cotter—Terry, from San Francisco, California, is the President of the International Travel Guild. He involved several Special Olympics athletes in World Ride. Terry participated on stages in Europe, Asia, and across the USA. He also took part in the first World T.E.A.M. Sports event, the Mt. Kilimanjaro climb.

Liza Engelbrecht—Liza lives in Durham, North Carolina, with her children Kelsey and Brit. Liza is a special events consultant for AXA World Ride '95. She joined several stages in Europe, Asia, and the USA.

John Fahner-Vihtelic—John is a technology licensing specialist for the National Institutes of Health in Bethesda, Maryland. John lost his left leg below the knee after a car accident in 1976.

Mary Ford—Mary lives in Jersey City, New Jersey, and is a Senior Program Consultant for The Equitable. Mary lost 100 pounds in preparation for World Ride '95.

Patrice Gaudin—Patrice, from Bassens, France, works for France Telecom. He rode as a tandem partner for a friend, Jean-Louis Gouzy, who is blind.

Jean-Louis Gouzy—Jean-Louis lives in Soturac, France. He has been blind since 1975. In tandem cycling he won seven French Championship titles and one World Championship title.

Janet Hass—Janet lives in Novato, California, and is a special education teacher at Novato High School. She has been a Special Olympics coach for 17 years. She brought Special Olympics athlete, Joelle Martin, with her on Stage Nine.

Laura Herrmann—Laura is a psychotherapist from Huntington, New York. She married David Cornelsen.

Eleanor Hogg—Eleanor quit her job as a medical sales representative to join the World T.E.A.M. Sports staff during World Ride '95. She resides in Walnut Creek, California, and works as a medical sales representative there.

Peter Kiernan—Peter is a partner with Goldman Sachs in New York City and was a founder of World T.E.A.M. Sports.

Thomas Lavalle—Tom lives in New Orleans, Louisiana, and is a senior architect with Capital Projects Administration. Tom has played semi-pro baseball, is a competitive triathlete, and has participated in several road and off-road rides. He volunteers with Special Olympics in Louisiana, where his younger sister, who has Down Syndrome, participates.

Joelle Martin—Joelle is a courtesy clerk for Long's Drugs in San Rafael, California. She is active in Special Olympics and came on World Ride with her coach and tandem partner, Janet Hass.

Chris Noonan—Chris lives in Dallas, Texas, where he is an agency manager for The Equitable. For several years he has coached swimming for persons with and without disabilities. He was a member of the crew team at Michigan State University. Chris volunteers with Special Olympics.

Robert Roark—Bob is a Professor of Pediatrics at the University of Colorado School of Medicine. Bob is a T12-L1 paraplegic who is very active in several sports. He and his wife Gruffie arrived early for Stage 9 to kayak in Mongolia.

Jane Schnell—Jane is a retired government worker living in Washington, D.C. She has written and published several books about bicycle touring. She celebrated her 65th birthday by participating in this ride.

Sergey Shestakov—Sergey was interpreter and guide for Stage 9. He was assisted by his daughter Jean Shestakov, a high school student in New York.

Bibliography

Burchert, Ulrich, & Roozongijin Enchbat, photoessay, *Mongolia —Country of Contrasts,* Ulaanbaatar, 1993.

DeWeck, Dr. Christine, *Siberia, Outer Mongolia, Central Asia: Crossroads of Civilization,* Vantage Press, Inc., New York, 1993.

Goldstein, Melvyn C., and Cynthia M. Beall, *The Changing World of Mongolia's Nomads,* University of California Press, Berkeley and Los Angeles, 1994.

Kuralt, Charles, host, *World Ride: The Possible Dream,* VHS-video, first shown on CBS, Thanksgiving Day, 1995.

Lattimore, Owen, *High Tartary,* Kodansha International, New York, 1994, Little, Brown, and Company, 1930.

Lincoln, W. Bruce, *The Conquest of a Continent—Siberia and the Russians,* Random House, New York, 1994.

Storey, Robert, *Mongolia—A Travel Survival Kit,* Lonely Planet Publications, Australia, 1993.

Tusltem, T., ed., Bayarsaikhan, D., *Mongolian Architecture,* State Publishing House, Ulan-Bator, 1988. (Text in English, French, Russian, Spanish.)

U.S. Department of State, *Background Notes—Mongolia,* GPO, October, 1993.

World T.E.A.M. Sports internal memos, newsletters: *One Voice,* and publications for World Ride participants, 1995-1996.

Yunden, Ya, Zorig, G., and Erdene, Ch., *This Is Mongolia,* UlaanBaatar, 1991.